THE MOBILE

Notary

BLUEPRINT

Launching and Managing Your On-Demand Business

DERRICK SPRUILL

Book edited by Lee Lee Trotter

Cover design, interior photos, and illustrations by Montes Travis

ISBN: 978-1-965-896-19-8

DEDICATION

This book is dedicated with a profound and hopeful heart to all those among us who are navigating the immense struggles of life, carrying burdens unseen, and who have not yet come to know the transformative love and unwavering peace of Jesus Christ.

May the diligence, integrity, and purpose found within these pages serve as a testament to the light that can illuminate any path. May the principles of service and trust, so central to the Notary Public office, inspire a deeper search for meaning and a connection to a higher calling.

It is my earnest prayer that, through the quiet pursuit of excellence in any endeavor, and by witnessing the steadfastness of faith in action, all who are searching may find solace, strength, and ultimately, the boundless grace that awaits them. May hope guide their steps, and may they come to know the profound peace that surpasses all understanding.

Legal Disclaimer:

The information provided in this book is for general informational and educational purposes only and is not intended to be a substitute for professional legal advice. While the author has made every effort to ensure the accuracy of the information, this book does not provide legal advice. Reading this book does not create an attorney-client relationship between the author and the reader. You should not act or refrain from acting based on any content included in this book without seeking legal or other professional advice. Readers are encouraged to consult with a qualified attorney licensed in their jurisdiction for advice specific to their individual circumstances. The author assumes no responsibility for errors or omissions, or for any damages that may result from the use of the information contained herein.

Table of Contents

Chapter 1: The Mobile Notary Revolution: Your Path to On-Demand Service

Hello, and welcome to **"The Mobile Notary Blueprint: Launching and Managing Your On-Demand Business."** I'm Derrick Spruill, and if you've followed my journey through Mobile Notary by Derrick Spruill, listened to my "Notary Knowledge by Derrick Spruill" podcast, or read my previous works like *Notary Knowledge: Reference Guide & Notary Bible*, you know my unwavering commitment to empowering notaries. This book, the fourth in our "Notary Knowledge: The Complete Guide Series," is where we shift gears from mastering the *act* of notarization to mastering the *business* of notarization. This is your essential guide to building a thriving mobile notary enterprise.

I. Introduction: Why Go Mobile? My Journey to On-Demand Notarization

For decades, the image of a notary public was often tied to a fixed location: a bank, a law office, or a courthouse. Clients expected to travel to the notary, often during limited business hours, and wait in line for a few moments of official service. But in today's fast-paced, convenience-driven world, that traditional model is rapidly evolving, and in many ways, being revolutionized. The demand for services that come directly to the client, on their schedule, at their preferred location, has not just grown; it has exploded. This profound shift in consumer expectation is the core of the **Mobile Notary Revolution**, and it represents your clear path to becoming an indispensable, highly sought-after, and truly on-demand professional.

My Personal Experience with Mobile Notary by Derrick Spruill: My own journey into the mobile notary world wasn't merely a calculated business decision; it was deeply personal and transformative. After years of dedicated leadership roles in demanding Fortune 100 companies, armed with the strategic insights from my MBA in Human Resources and the analytical precision from my bachelor's degree in accounting from Walden University, I found myself at a crossroads. My extensive corporate experience, spanning over 25 years, had honed my business acumen, my ability to navigate complex operational challenges, and my profound passion for helping others, particularly in addressing intricate human resource issues and handling sensitive documents with utmost care. Yet, despite the satisfaction of my corporate career, I knew I wanted to contribute more directly, to build something tangible that directly served individuals in their most critical moments of need.

I often reflect on a pivotal, deeply impactful moment that truly illuminated this path for me. It was about ten years ago that an incident occurred in Norfolk, Virginia. My wife and I were at a local hospital on a Saturday morning, facing a stressful and urgent situation: we desperately needed a notary for my ailing mother-in-law. We searched frantically, we called numerous offices, but we simply could not find anyone available to help us in that great time of need, especially on a weekend. It was, without exaggeration, one of the most stressful 48 hours of our lives, filled with anxiety and helplessness over an urgent legal document that needed immediate attention. (Thankfully, my mother-in-law is still with us today, a testament to God's grace and a constant reminder of that challenging time.) That experience burned a profound question into my mind: *Why should anyone go through that stress and anxiety, unable to acquire a service they desperately need in moments of uncertainty or vulnerability, simply because it's after hours or they can't travel?*

That was my "lightbulb moment." I realized I could fill that critical void. I could leverage my existing expertise in handling sensitive documents, my corporate background in operational efficiency, and my deep-seated desire to serve, to become a Notary Public who conducted traveling services—a dedicated mobile notary. The thought ignited a fire within me: "I can fill my time studying this craft, become a master at it, and be my very own boss. I could travel to places I never traveled before and meet people I never knew. This could be fulfilling." (As I shared in my first entrepreneurial guide, *Quick & Easy Solutions: How to Increase Mobile Notary Business for More Success & Profit*, published in 2023). That singular moment of personal need and frustration transformed directly into the mission and driving force behind Mobile Notary by Derrick Spruill. It became my personal commitment to ensure others wouldn't face the same struggle.

The Growing Demand for Convenience: The world has undergone a profound shift towards on-demand services, driven by busy lifestyles and technological advancements. We now routinely expect food delivered to our door, groceries picked up and ready for collection, and a vast array of services available at our fingertips through apps and online platforms. Notarization is no different; it has become an integral part of this convenience economy. People are busier than ever, often juggling demanding careers, complex family responsibilities, and numerous personal commitments. They value their time, flexibility, and convenience above almost all else. The traditional model of taking precious time off work, battling relentless traffic, endlessly searching for parking, and enduring frustrating waits in line at a bank or a shipping store is increasingly seen as an unacceptable inconvenience. This escalating demand for accessible, on-location services creates a massive and ever-growing opportunity for mobile notaries who can bring the essential service directly to the client, on their terms, wherever and whenever it's needed. This trend is not a fleeting fad; it's a fundamental change in how services are consumed.

What This Book Will Empower You To Do: This book, "The Mobile Notary Blueprint," is your comprehensive, step-by-step guide. I will meticulously guide you through every critical stage of launching, establishing, and successfully managing your own profitable and highly respected mobile notary business. By the end of this journey, you will be equipped with the knowledge and confidence to:

- **Structure your business legally and financially:** Understand the vital decisions regarding business entities, licenses, permits, and banking that protect your personal assets and ensure compliance from day one.
- **Equip your mobile office for on-the-go excellence:** Learn precisely what tools and technologies are essential for efficient, professional, and secure notarizations wherever your clients may be.
- **Price your services strategically for profit and competitiveness:** Discover how to value your time, calculate your costs, and set fees that attract clients while ensuring your business thrives financially.
- **Master efficient scheduling and logistics:** Optimize your routes, manage your calendar, and streamline your operations to maximize billable hours and minimize unproductive time.
- **Attract and retain a loyal client base through effective marketing:** Build a powerful online presence, cultivate robust referral networks, and implement direct client acquisition strategies that ensure a steady stream of business.
- **Provide truly exceptional customer service that sets you apart:** Learn how to deliver an unparalleled client experience

that fosters loyalty, generates glowing reviews, and turns satisfied clients into enthusiastic advocates for your business.

II. The Mobile Notary Advantage: Benefits Redefined

Becoming a mobile notary isn't just about starting another business; it's about embracing a dynamic service model that offers profound and transformative advantages for both your clients and your own professional growth and entrepreneurial aspirations. It's a win-win scenario that drives the revolution.

For the Client: Unparalleled Convenience and Accessibility: The appeal of mobile notary services for clients is undeniable and multifaceted. It's about making their lives significantly easier, reducing their stress, and ensuring they can access vital legal and financial services precisely when and where they need them, without compromise.

- **Time-Saving and Flexibility of Location (Home, Office, Hospital):** This is, without question, the most significant and universally appreciated benefit for clients. They are entirely freed from the arduous and often frustrating tasks of commuting, battling traffic, endlessly searching for elusive parking, and enduring unpredictable waits. I bring the service directly to them, whether it's their private residence for sensitive estate documents, their bustling corporate office for urgent business contracts, or a hospital or nursing home for critical medical directives. This unparalleled flexibility means notarization fits seamlessly into *their* demanding schedule, saving them invaluable time, dramatically reducing their stress levels, and allowing them to focus on more important matters. I've personally traveled to clients who needed documents notarized at 2:00 AM in a hospital after a car accident, or even before a wedding reception at a hotel for a last-minute vehicle purchase (as I recount in *Quick & Easy Solutions*). These are not mere conveniences; they are moments where on-demand service is not just a luxury, but a critical necessity that can avert major problems.

- **Increased Privacy and Personalized Service:** Notarizing highly sensitive documents (such as wills, trusts, divorce settlements, or confidential business agreements) in a private, familiar, and comfortable environment (like their own home or a secluded office meeting room) is far more comfortable, discreet, and less intimidating for clients than conducting such personal business in a bustling, public setting like a crowded bank lobby or a busy shipping store. My service offers a dedicated, one-on-one interaction, allowing for thorough ID verification, patient guidance through the notarial process (without offering legal advice), and fostering a deeper sense of trust and personalized attention. This tailored approach respects the sensitive nature of many notarized documents and contributes to a more relaxed and positive experience.
- **Crucial Access for Vulnerable Populations (Elderly, Disabled, Remote):** This is truly where the mobile notary makes a profound and often life-changing difference, embodying the spirit of public service. For elderly individuals with limited mobility, homebound clients due to illness or disability, or those residing in geographically remote areas with sparse notary services, a mobile notary provides essential, often life-saving, access to critical legal functions they might otherwise be entirely unable to obtain. I've had the distinct honor of traveling deep into the Appalachian Mountains to a client's secluded home, a "little piece of heaven," to notarize documents for someone who had lived there all his life and simply couldn't travel. As I reflected after that deeply moving visit, "I think about how many of us are so privileged to go about our day taking instant access and mobility for granted... when I can help others in their time of need, I try my best to help others by bending over backward and going that extra mile whenever I can." (This powerful sentiment is echoed in Chapter 2 of *Quick & Easy Solutions*). This unwavering commitment to accessibility and dignity is a powerful and constant motivator for me, highlighting the profound human impact of mobile notary services.

For the Notary: Entrepreneurial Opportunity and Professional Growth: Offering mobile services isn't just about providing benefits to clients; it's about building a dynamic, flexible, and financially rewarding business for yourself, transforming your commission into a powerful entrepreneurial engine.

- **Increased Earning Potential and Greater Financial Control:** This is one of the most tangible and attractive benefits. Mobile notaries are legitimately permitted to charge a separate travel fee in addition to the per-signature notary fee (where allowed by state law). This travel fee directly compensates you for your valuable time spent driving, mileage, and vehicle wear and tear, significantly increasing your income potential compared to basic, walk-in notarizations. Furthermore, offering specialized services (like loan signings or apostille services, as discussed in *Notary Niche Navigator*) allows you to command significantly higher flat fees, reflecting the increased complexity and value. As an independent mobile notary, you gain direct control over your pricing structure (within state limits), your service offerings, and your overall work volume, directly impacting your earning potential and fostering greater financial autonomy. This allows you to scale your income based on your effort and strategic choices.
- **Unparalleled Flexibility and Autonomy (Being Your Own Boss):** This is a huge draw for many professionals. As an independent mobile notary, you gain the freedom to set your own hours, choosing precisely when and how much you work. This unparalleled flexibility allows you to balance notary work with other professional commitments, family responsibilities, personal pursuits, or even other entrepreneurial ventures. It provides the freedom to decline jobs that don't fit your schedule or profitability goals, giving you genuine control over your work-life balance. You are building *your* business, on *your* terms.
- **Expanded Client Base and Broader Market Reach:** By actively traveling to clients, you can reach a significantly broader and more diverse client base than traditional walk-in

notaries confined to a fixed location. You can tap into previously underserved markets (e.g., rural areas, specific industries, after-hours clients) and build robust, sustainable referral networks with key professionals like real estate agents, attorneys, title companies, and hospital administrators. My own business, Mobile Notary by Derrick Spruill, proudly serves Loudoun, Fairfax, and Prince William Counties in Northern Virginia, reaching a wide and diverse demographic that values convenience. This broad reach translates directly into more consistent business opportunities.

- **Accelerated Professional Growth and Specialization:** The diverse range of documents encountered, the varied client interactions, and the logistical challenges inherent in mobile notarization contribute to rapid and profound professional growth. You'll gain exposure to a wider array of legal documents and learn to adapt to different environments and unexpected situations. This naturally leads to specialization, such as becoming a highly skilled Loan Signing Agent (LSA), which further enhances your marketability, allows you to command premium fees, and positions you as a respected authority in your chosen niche. This continuous learning and adaptation keeps your skills sharp and your business relevant in an evolving professional landscape.

III. Assessing Your Readiness: Are You Prepared for Mobile Notary Work?

While the advantages of a mobile notary business are compelling and numerous, embarking on this entrepreneurial path requires a realistic and honest self-assessment. It's not for everyone, and your ultimate success hinges on a blend of specific personal attributes, a rock-solid foundational knowledge, and a disciplined mindset regarding initial investments.

Personal Attributes: Self-Motivation, Professionalism, Adaptability:

- **Self-Motivation & Discipline:** As your own boss, you are entirely responsible for your success. There's no one to tell you to get out of bed for that 4:00 AM call (as I've personally experienced, as detailed in *Quick & Easy Solutions*!). You need immense self-motivation, discipline, and initiative to manage your time effectively, proactively market your services, stay compliant with regulations, and consistently deliver high-quality work without external oversight.
- **Professionalism & Poise:** You are the direct face of your business. Impeccable professionalism, a calm and reassuring demeanor, and excellent communication skills are absolutely non-negotiable. You will encounter diverse personalities, varying levels of client stress, and sometimes challenging situations. Your ability to maintain composure, project confidence, and conduct yourself with dignity in every interaction is paramount to building trust and a stellar reputation.
- **Adaptability & Problem-Solving:** Mobile work, by its very nature, is unpredictable. You might face unexpected traffic delays, difficult parking situations, a client who is unprepared, or unforeseen document issues on-site. The ability to adapt quickly, problem-solve calmly under pressure, think on your feet, and maintain composure when things don't go as planned

is crucial for delivering seamless service and preventing minor issues from escalating into major problems.

- **Empathy & Compassion (Balanced with Impartiality):** As I shared in Chapter 2 of *Quick & Easy Solutions*, sometimes a notary call comes from a hospital in the middle of the night for an injured person, or from a family dealing with a sensitive estate matter. Showing genuine empathy and compassion for your clients' situations, while always remaining impartial in your official duties, is vital. My experiences have taught me that "Possess the correct emotional IQ for each type of situation so you will be a correct lasting response to the moment." This balance of human connection and professional detachment is a fine art.

Foundational Knowledge: Understanding Your State's Notary Laws (Recap from *The Notary Public Foundation*):

- Before you even *think* about going mobile or marketing your services, you must possess a rock-solid, comprehensive understanding of your state's specific notary laws and regulations. This foundational knowledge is your first and most critical line of defense against errors, liability, and fraud. This includes, but is not limited to:
  - Acceptable forms of identification and rigorous verification procedures.
  - The distinct purposes and proper procedures for Acknowledgments, Jurats, and Oaths/Affirmations.
  - Meticulous journal keeping requirements and secure storage protocols.
  - Precise rules for notary seals and approved ink colors.
  - Strict prohibitions (especially the Unauthorized Practice of Law - UPL, as detailed in *Notary Fraud Shield*).
- Your state's official notary handbook is your bible, and continuous learning is paramount. If you haven't thoroughly absorbed the content from *The Notary Public Foundation*, I urge you to do so, as it provides the indispensable legal framework for all your operations.

Initial Investment Mindset: Time, Training, and Equipment:

- **Time:** Be prepared to invest significant time upfront. This includes time for in-depth research, formal business setup, developing your marketing strategies, and potentially completing specialized training (e.g., Loan Signing Agent certification, Remote Online Notarization commissioning). This is an investment in your future earning potential.
- **Training:** While your basic notary commission provides foundational authority (covered in *The Notary Public Foundation*), successful mobile notary work often benefits immensely from additional, specialized training. This might include courses in loan signings, specific RON platform training, advanced fraud detection, or even small business management. These specialized skills open doors to higher-paying niches.
- **Equipment:** You'll need to make a prudent initial investment in essential equipment. This ranges from a reliable, well-maintained vehicle to a professional-grade printer/scanner, a mobile hotspot for connectivity, and your core notary supplies (as detailed in Chapter 3 of this book, *The Mobile Notary Blueprint*). This is not a zero-cost venture; view these as necessary tools for delivering professional, efficient, and secure service.

Conclusion

The mobile notary revolution is not just a trend; it's a dynamic and expanding opportunity for those willing to embrace its demands and responsibilities. My journey, from a pivotal moment in a Norfolk hospital to building and growing Mobile Notary by Derrick Spruill in Herndon, Virginia, has shown me the immense value, profound satisfaction, and significant potential of serving clients on-demand. By truly understanding the unparalleled advantages for both your clients and yourself, and by honestly assessing your readiness—embracing self-motivation, honing your professionalism, committing to continuous learning, and making the necessary strategic investments—you can confidently embark on this rewarding path.

This book, "The Mobile Notary Blueprint," will be your comprehensive guide as you launch, manage, and scale your own successful on-demand notary business, transforming your commission into a powerful engine for service, profit, and a lasting legacy of trust.

Chapter 2: Laying the Foundation: Legal, Financial, and Insurance Setup

Welcome to "The Mobile Notary Blueprint." In Chapter 1, I shared my journey into the mobile notary revolution and explored the compelling advantages of offering on-demand services. Now that you're inspired to build your own mobile notary business, it's time to get down to the critical details of **laying a solid foundation**. Just as a skyscraper needs deep, stable footings and a robust structural framework before its walls can rise, your mobile notary business requires proper legal, financial, and insurance structures. Skipping these essential setup steps, or doing them incorrectly, can lead to significant headaches, expose you to unforeseen legal vulnerabilities, and create substantial financial risks down the road. My own experience, leveraging the strategic insights from my MBA in Human Resources and the analytical precision from my accounting background from Walden University, taught me the absolute necessity of meticulous planning and diligent execution from day one in any business venture. This chapter will meticulously guide you through these essential setup steps, ensuring your mobile notary business is built on solid, compliant, and protected ground, ready for sustainable growth.

I. Introduction: Building on Solid Ground

When I first decided to launch Mobile Notary by Derrick Spruill, I understood intuitively that my profound passion for serving others had to be matched by equally sound and rigorous business practices. My years working for Fortune 100 companies instilled in me a deep appreciation for robust operational foundations; I saw firsthand how even minor structural weaknesses could lead to cascading problems for large organizations. The same principle applies, perhaps even more critically, to a small, independent business like a mobile notary service. You simply cannot consistently provide excellent customer service, meticulously prevent fraud (as explored in *Notary Fraud Shield*), or ensure unwavering compliance if your own underlying business structure is shaky or unprotected. My approach has always been to build on solid ground, prioritizing legal compliance and personal protection from the outset. This initial setup phase is precisely where you transform your notary commission from a personal credential into a legitimate, resilient, and professionally recognized business entity capable of long-term success. It's the moment you establish the formal identity of your enterprise.

II. Structuring Your Business: Choosing the Right Legal Entity

One of the very first and most critical decisions you'll make as you embark on your mobile notary journey is choosing the legal structure for your business. This foundational choice profoundly impacts your personal liability (how much of your personal wealth is at risk), your tax obligations (how your business income is taxed), and your administrative burden (the paperwork and compliance required). As I shared in *Quick & Easy Solutions: How to Increase Mobile Notary Business for More Success & Profit*, "I cannot advise you on which one to choose, but once you select it, you can proceed to the next step. I am not an attorney, and I do not have a law degree, so none of the information is meant to be considered legal advice." However, I can explain the common options and their practical implications for a mobile notary, guiding your research with legal and financial professionals.

Sole Proprietorship: Simplicity vs. Unlimited Liability:

- **Description:** This is the simplest and most common legal structure for individuals starting a small business, particularly if they are the sole owner. In a sole proprietorship, there is no legal distinction between you, the individual owner, and your business. You are personally responsible for all aspects of the business.
- **Pros:** It's the easiest and least expensive structure to set up, often requiring minimal legal formalities beyond obtaining your notary commission and any local business licenses. For tax purposes, profits and losses are reported directly on your personal tax return (using Schedule C, Profit or Loss from Business), simplifying filing.
- **Cons:** The most significant and potentially devastating drawback is **no personal liability protection**. This means your personal assets (your home, personal savings, investment accounts, personal vehicle) are directly and entirely at risk if your business incurs debts, faces a lawsuit (e.g., due to a notary error or negligence), or encounters other financial liabilities. A judgment against your business is a judgment against you personally, potentially leading to the seizure of your personal property. For a notary, given the inherent risks of the profession (as detailed in *Notary Fraud Shield* and *Notary Law & Liability*), this is a substantial and often unacceptable risk.

Limited Liability Company (LLC): Balancing Robust Protection and Operational Simplicity:

- **Description:** An LLC is a hybrid business structure that ingeniously combines the personal liability protection typically associated with a corporation with the tax benefits and operational simplicity often found in a sole proprietorship or partnership. It creates a formal legal separation between you, the owner (or "member"), and your business entity.

- **Pros:** This is a very popular and often highly recommended choice for mobile notaries due to its advantageous balance. An LLC provides **personal liability protection**, legally shielding your personal assets from most business debts, lawsuits, and other liabilities. If your LLC is sued, generally, only the assets owned by the LLC itself are at risk, not your personal wealth. This offers immense peace of mind. Furthermore, an LLC often lends more credibility and a more professional image to clients and crucial professional partners (like title companies or law firms) than a sole proprietorship. Tax flexibility is another significant advantage, as an LLC can elect to be taxed in various ways (e.g., as a disregarded entity like a sole proprietorship, a partnership, or even an S-Corporation), allowing for tax optimization as your business grows.
- **Cons:** It is more complex and costly to set up and maintain than a sole proprietorship. This involves state filing fees (for formation and often annual reports), potentially registered agent fees (a third party designated to receive legal documents on behalf of your LLC), and requires more administrative upkeep (e.g., maintaining an operating agreement, keeping separate business records, and ensuring strict separation of personal and business finances to avoid "piercing the corporate veil").

- **C. Other Structures (Briefly: Partnership, Corporation): Partnership:** This structure is suitable if you plan to operate your mobile notary business jointly with one or more partners. A formal partnership agreement is crucial, outlining responsibilities, profit-sharing arrangements, and dispute

resolution mechanisms. However, general partnerships typically involve shared and often unlimited liability for all partners, meaning each partner can be held personally responsible for the partnership's debts and actions. Limited Partnerships (LPs) or Limited Liability Partnerships (LLPs) offer some liability protection but are more complex.

- **Corporation (S-Corp, C-Corp):** While corporations offer the strongest form of personal liability protection, they are generally considered overkill and unnecessarily complex for a single mobile notary or even a small notary team. They involve significant setup costs, rigorous legal formalities (e.g., bylaws, regular board meetings, detailed minutes, separate corporate tax returns), and extensive ongoing compliance requirements. They might only be considered if you plan to scale significantly, raise substantial outside capital, or bring on numerous employees, or if a tax accountant identifies very specific, significant tax advantages for your unique financial situation that outweigh the administrative burden.

Key Considerations for Your Choice (Liability, Taxes, Credibility, Administrative Burden): As I emphasized in *Quick & Easy Solutions*, "There are great benefits between these structures, so please conduct your due diligence in researching the difference and choose wisely in the beginning because it may cost you time and money later to make these changes." Your decision should carefully weigh these interconnected factors:

- **Personal Liability Protection:** This is paramount for notaries. How much personal financial risk are you comfortable with? An LLC offers a robust shield that a sole proprietorship does not. Consider the potential for lawsuits related to notary errors (as detailed in *Notary Fraud Shield* and *Notary Law & Liability*).
- **Tax Implications:** How will each structure affect your income taxes, self-employment taxes, and potential deductions? This is where consulting a qualified accountant is invaluable. They can advise on the most tax-efficient structure for your projected income and expenses.
- **Credibility and Professional Image:** How do you want your business to be perceived by clients and potential partners (e.g., title companies, law firms)? An LLC often conveys more professionalism and seriousness than a sole proprietorship, which can be crucial for attracting higher-value business.
- **Administrative Burden and Cost:** How much time, effort, and money are you willing to invest in ongoing compliance, record-keeping, and annual filings? Sole proprietorships are minimal, while LLCs require more, and corporations significantly more. Factor in state filing fees and potential professional service fees (accountant, registered agent).

III. Essential Legal & Administrative Registrations

Once you've made the pivotal decision on your business structure, the next crucial phase involves completing the necessary legal and administrative registrations. These steps formalize your business's existence, establish its legal identity, and ensure you're operating compliantly with various governmental levels, preventing unexpected fines and legal issues down the line.

Choosing and Registering Your Business Name:

- **Professionalism and Memorability:** Selecting a compelling business name is a critical branding decision that impacts your market perception. Choose a name that is professional, easy to remember, and clearly indicates the services you provide. Aim for something that conveys trust, reliability, and convenience, reflecting the core values of your mobile notary service. As I asked myself when launching Mobile Notary by Derrick Spruill, "Simple, straightforward. It works, putting the pressure on myself to live up to integrity in being the best. Who wants to associate their name with subpar?" Your name becomes your promise.
- **Availability Check (Multi-Layered and Thorough):** Before finalizing your chosen name, it is absolutely meticulous to check for its availability across multiple platforms to avoid future conflicts and ensure brand consistency. This involves:
    - **State Level:** Verify if the exact name is available for registration with your state's Secretary of State (or equivalent agency) for your chosen business entity type (e.g., LLC registration). This is usually the first legal check.
    - **Federal Trademarks:** Conduct a basic search on the U.S. Patent and Trademark Office (USPTO) website to ensure your chosen name isn't already federally trademarked by another business, especially in related service categories. This prevents future legal disputes over intellectual property.
    - **Online Presence:** Crucially, ensure the corresponding website domain name (e.g., `yourbusinessname.com`, `.net`, `.org`) is available for purchase. Also, check for availability of relevant social media handles (e.g., LinkedIn, Facebook, Instagram, X) to maintain brand

consistency across your entire digital footprint (as discussed in Chapter 6 of *The Mobile Notary Blueprint*).

- **Professional Email Domain:** Once you secure your business name and website domain, establish a professional email address using your domain (e.g., `yourname@yourbusinessname.com` or `info@yourbusinessname.com`). This instantly enhances your credibility and professionalism in every communication, distinguishing you from generic email addresses and reinforcing your brand identity.

Obtaining Necessary State and Local Business Licenses & Permits:

- Beyond your fundamental notary commission (which is a state-level public office appointment), operating a legitimate business requires adherence to additional legal authorizations at various governmental levels. These requirements vary widely and are highly localized by city, town, and county. It is absolutely crucial to check meticulously with your local city hall, county clerk's office, or municipal business licensing department for any required general business licenses, specific occupational permits (e.g., for mobile services or home-based businesses), or local business taxes specific to operating a mobile notary service in your area. Some residential zones may have specific requirements or restrictions for home-based businesses, even if clients don't visit your home. Failing to obtain these can result in fines and legal issues.

Securing an Employer Identification Number (EIN):

- **Purpose:** An EIN is a unique nine-digit tax identification number assigned by the IRS (Internal Revenue Service). It functions like a Social Security Number but is specifically for your business, allowing the IRS to identify your business for tax purposes. It's essential for various financial and legal activities.

- **When Needed:** You will absolutely need an EIN if you form an LLC (even if you're the only member), if you plan to hire any employees (even part-time administrative help), or if you elect to operate as a corporation or partnership. Even as a sole proprietor without employees, many banks require an EIN to open a dedicated business bank account, and it simplifies tax reporting by separating your personal and business tax identities.
- **How to Get It:** You can apply for an EIN for free directly on the IRS website. The application process is straightforward, typically takes only a few minutes, and the EIN is usually issued immediately. Be cautious of third-party services that charge a fee for this free government service.

Opening a Dedicated Business Bank Account (Crucial for Legal and Financial Separation):

- **Crucial for Separation and Compliance:** This is a non-negotiable and foundational step for maintaining professionalism, simplifying your financial management, and, critically, protecting your personal assets, especially if you operate as an LLC. As I reflected in *Quick & Easy Solutions*, "On October 9th, we went to the bank with our documents to open a business checking and savings account with the official business name. That was an exciting day." This was a pivotal moment for establishing my business's formal identity.
- **Benefits:**
    - **Legal Protection and "Piercing the Corporate Veil":** If you're operating as an LLC, a separate business bank account is absolutely vital to reinforce the legal separation between your personal and business finances. "Commingling" of funds (mixing personal and business money) is a primary reason courts might "pierce the corporate veil" of an LLC, making the owner personally liable for business debts—exactly what the LLC was designed to prevent. Maintaining distinct accounts demonstrates that your business is a separate legal entity.

- **Simplified Tax Preparation and Audits:** Keeping all business income and expenses separate from personal funds makes tracking your finances significantly easier for tax purposes. It streamlines the process of preparing your annual tax returns (e.g., filling out Schedule C for sole proprietorships/LLCs taxed as such) and makes audits by the IRS far less complicated, as your business finances are clearly delineated and verifiable.
- **Enhanced Professionalism and Credibility:** Presenting clients with a business bank account for payments, using business checks, accepting credit card payments through a business merchant account, or sending professional invoices gives a far more professional and credible image than using a personal account. This signals that you operate a legitimate, organized business, which builds trust with clients and potential referral partners.
- **Budgeting and Financial Management:** A separate account helps you effectively manage business cash flow, track profitability, analyze expenses, and make informed financial decisions for your mobile notary practice. It provides a clear, accurate picture of your business's financial health, allowing you to monitor income, control spending, and plan for future investments.

III. Insurance and Bonding: Protecting Your Business and Yourself

While your state-mandated notary bond primarily protects the public, you need additional, crucial insurance to protect your business and personal assets from the inherent and significant risks of the notary profession. This comprehensive approach to risk management is your personal financial shield, safeguarding you from potentially devastating lawsuits and claims.

Notary Bond (Mandatory in Many States):

- **Purpose:** This is a surety bond required by many states (refer to Chapter 4 of *The Notary Public Foundation* for your state's specific requirements and Chapter 29 of *Notary Knowledge: Reference Guide & Notary Bible* for a detailed state-by-state list). Its fundamental purpose is to provide a financial safety net for the `public` (the citizens of the state) who may suffer financial harm or loss directly caused by a notary's official misconduct, negligence, or errors in performing their duties.
- **How it Works (Three-Party Agreement):** A notary bond involves three distinct parties:
    1. **Principal:** The Notary Public (you). You are the individual whose performance is being guaranteed.
    2. **Obligee:** The State (which requires the bond). The state is the entity to whom the promise of performance is made, acting on behalf of its citizens to ensure they are protected.
    3. **Surety:** The bonding company (which issues the bond). This is a financial institution that guarantees the notary's performance up to the bond amount. If a valid claim is made against the bond due to the notary's error, the surety company pays the injured party.
- **Crucial Distinction: Not Insurance for the Notary:** It is absolutely critical for every notary to understand that a notary bond is `not` insurance for the notary. If a valid claim is paid from your bond due to your error or misconduct, the surety company (the bonding company) will then seek full reimbursement from you (the notary, as the "Principal" of the bond) for the entire amount paid out. This legal right of the surety company is called `indemnification`, meaning you are ultimately responsible for the damages you cause. The bond simply ensures that the injured party has a readily available source of funds for compensation, rather than having to sue the notary directly and potentially find them judgment-proof.
- **Bond Amounts and Their Limitations:** Bond amounts vary significantly by state, typically ranging from a low of $500 to a high of $25,000. These amounts are often relatively small

compared to the potential financial damages that can arise from a notary's error, particularly in high-value transactions like real estate closings (which can involve hundreds of thousands or millions of dollars). This disparity highlights the critical need for additional protection beyond the bond. For example, a $15,000 bond would barely cover the legal fees, let alone the damages, in a major real estate fraud case.

Errors & Omissions (E&O) Insurance (Highly Recommended and Often Indispensable):

- **Purpose:** While a notary bond is a state-mandated protection for the public, `Errors & Omissions (E&O) insurance` is professional liability insurance that directly protects the notary themselves. It is arguably the single most important financial safeguard a notary can have, especially for those operating as mobile notaries or Loan Signing Agents who frequently handle high-value transactions. E&O insurance acts as your personal financial shield against the potentially ruinous costs of lawsuits and claims.
- **How E&O Insurance Works: Your Personal Financial Safeguard:**
    - **Coverage for Legal Defense Costs:** This is often the most significant and immediate benefit of E&O insurance. Even if a claim against you is frivolous, baseless, or you are ultimately found not liable, defending against a lawsuit can be incredibly expensive, quickly accumulating tens of thousands of dollars in legal fees. E&O insurance covers attorney fees, court costs, investigation expenses, and other legal expenses incurred in your defense, up to the policy limit. Without E&O, these costs would come directly out of your personal pocket, potentially leading to financial ruin.
    - **Coverage for Judgments and Settlements:** If you are found legally liable for damages in a civil lawsuit or if a settlement is reached out of court, the E&O policy pays out the compensation to the injured party, up to

its coverage limit. This is what truly protects your personal assets (e.g., home, savings, investments) from being seized to satisfy a judgment.

- **Why It's Indispensable (Beyond the Bond):**
    - **Bond Insufficiency:** As noted, notary bond amounts are often far too low to cover the full extent of damages in a major lawsuit (e.g., a fraudulent real estate transaction that could involve hundreds of thousands or millions of dollars). E&O insurance provides crucial coverage `beyond` the bond amount, acting as your primary line of defense against catastrophic financial loss.
    - **Defense Costs Coverage:** The notary bond does not cover your legal defense costs. E&O insurance does. This is a critical distinction, as legal defense fees can quickly deplete personal savings even for claims that are ultimately dismissed.
    - **Peace of Mind:** Knowing that you have robust E&O coverage provides crucial peace of mind, allowing you to focus on performing your duties diligently and professionally without the constant fear of personal financial ruin from an unforeseen error or a baseless claim.
    - **Professional Credibility and Access to High-Value Work:** Carrying E&O insurance demonstrates a high level of professionalism, responsibility, and commitment to client protection. Many signing services, title companies, and legal firms prefer or even `require` their notaries to carry specific E&O coverage limits (e.g., $100,000 or more) as a condition of hiring for high-value loan signings or legal document work.
- **Coverage Limits: Choosing Wisely:** E&O policies are available in various coverage limits (e.g., $25,000, $50,000, $100,000, $250,000, $500,000, $1,000,000). Notaries should purchase coverage sufficient to protect their personal assets and commensurate with the value and risk profile of documents they typically notarize. For instance, a notary who only notarizes simple affidavits for $5 might be comfortable

with a lower limit, but a Loan Signing Agent who regularly handles real estate transactions worth hundreds of thousands or millions of dollars should carry a much higher limit (e.g., $100,000 or more is strongly recommended for LSAs). The higher the potential value of the documents you handle, the higher your E&O coverage should be to adequately protect you.
- **Cost:** The annual premium for E&O insurance is relatively inexpensive compared to the potentially ruinous financial risks it mitigates. It is a small, but vital, investment for substantial personal and professional protection.

General Liability Insurance (Important Consideration for Mobile Notaries):

- **Purpose:** Also known as "business liability insurance" or "commercial general liability (CGL)," this type of insurance protects your business against claims of bodily injury or property damage that might occur to a third party (e.g., a client, a bystander) while you are conducting your business operations. It covers incidents unrelated to the notarial act itself.
- **Why It's Relevant for Mobile Notaries:** As a mobile notary, you frequently travel to clients' homes, offices, or other locations, entering various environments. This inherently involves risk. General liability insurance could provide crucial coverage if, for example, a client trips over your notary bag in their home and injures themselves, or if you accidentally spill coffee on a client's expensive rug or electronic equipment. It complements E&O by covering non-notarial incidents.
- **Scope:** It typically covers third-party claims for bodily injury, property damage, and sometimes personal and advertising injury (e.g., libel or slander).

Commercial Auto Insurance (Crucial Consideration for Business Use):

- **Purpose:** Standard personal auto insurance policies are typically designed for personal use and may explicitly exclude coverage for accidents or damages that occur while you are using your vehicle primarily for business purposes (e.g., driving to and from notary appointments, transporting business equipment).
- **Why It's Relevant for Mobile Notaries:** If you use your personal vehicle extensively for your mobile notary business, it is absolutely crucial to consult your auto insurance provider. You may need to add a "commercial rider" to your existing personal policy or obtain a separate commercial auto policy to ensure you are fully covered for business-related driving activities. Failure to do so could result in denied claims in the event of an accident during a work-related trip, leaving you personally responsible for vehicle damage, medical bills, and liability claims. This is a significant risk for any mobile professional.

IV. Initial Equipment and Supplies Investment: Building Your Mobile Office Foundation

Being meticulously well-equipped is paramount for a mobile notary. Having the right tools ensures efficiency, compliance, professionalism, and the ability to handle diverse client needs on every assignment. This section focuses on the *initial strategic investment* in equipment and supplies when first setting up your mobile notary business. Think of this as establishing the core foundation of your portable command center, rather than a comprehensive list of every single item (which is covered in detail in Chapter 19 of *Notary Knowledge: Reference Guide & Notary Bible*).

Core Notary Essentials (Mandatory Initial Purchases): These are the fundamental instruments you *must* acquire immediately after your commission is active and filed. They are non-negotiable for performing any legal notarial act.

- **Official Notary Seal/Stamp:** Your unique, state-compliant notary seal is your primary tool of authority. You'll need to purchase one that adheres to your state's specific design, content, and ink color requirements (refer to Chapter 9 of *Notary Operational Excellence*). This is a foundational purchase that legally authenticates your acts.
- **Notary Journal:** A bound, tamper-evident notary journal is typically a legally mandated record-keeping tool. You'll need to acquire one that complies with your state's specific format and entry requirements (refer to Chapter 2 of *Notary Operational Excellence*). This is crucial for establishing your audit trail from day one.
- **High-Quality Pens:** Invest in a set of reliable, permanent, non-smearing pens in approved ink colors (usually dark blue or black, as per Chapter 3 of *Notary Operational Excellence*). These are essential for your signature, the signer's signature, and completing certificates and journal entries.
- **Basic Loose Notarial Certificates:** While documents often come with pre-printed certificates, it's wise to have a small supply of blank, state-compliant loose certificates (e.g.,

Acknowledgments, Jurats) on hand. These are inexpensive but vital for situations where a document lacks a certificate or has incorrect wording.

- **State Notary Handbook:** Keep a physical copy of your state's official notary handbook or a quick reference guide easily accessible. This is your primary legal reference for confirming procedures and laws on the go.

Foundational Mobile Office Technology (Strategic Initial Investments): For a mobile notary, technology is key to efficiency and expanding services. These are initial investments to consider for your mobile operations.

- **Reliable Laptop or Tablet:** A portable computing device is essential for managing your business. It allows you to access electronic documents, manage your schedule, communicate with clients, and is fundamental if you plan to pursue Remote Online Notarization (RON) or Electronic Notarization (eNotary).
- **Mobile Hotspot or Reliable Internet Access:** Consistent internet connectivity is crucial for a mobile business. An initial investment in a dedicated mobile hotspot device or ensuring your smartphone's data plan supports reliable tethering will be vital for accessing online resources, communication, and digital notarization platforms.
- **Basic Portable Printer/Scanner (Consider for Efficiency):** While not strictly mandatory for *every* notary, an initial investment in a compact, battery-powered portable printer/scanner can significantly enhance efficiency, especially if you anticipate handling loan signings or general notary work requiring on-site printing or scanning. This can be a phased investment.
- **GPS/Navigation:** A reliable GPS device or a smartphone with up-to-date navigation apps is essential for efficient route planning, finding client locations, and ensuring punctuality.

Initial Payment Processing Setup: Setting up your payment acceptance methods from the start ensures you can get paid efficiently and professionally.

- **Mobile Card Reader:** Invest in a mobile card reader (e.g., Square, PayPal Here) that connects to your smartphone. This allows you to accept credit/debit card payments on the spot, offering convenience to clients and improving your cash flow. My experience with Square has been incredibly positive; as I noted in *Quick & Easy Solutions*, "We have enjoyed such great benefits from using Square over the years. Easy to use by tap, dip, or swipe. Recently, we can now use the tap feature with the RF or RFID or radio frequency contactless credit card software without the hardware directly on our phone." This ease of payment is a significant customer service advantage.
- **Basic Invoicing/Receipt System:** Set up a simple invoicing app or purchase a physical receipt book to provide professional, itemized receipts for all services rendered.

V. Initial Marketing and Branding Setup: Getting Discovered

Even with the best tools and legal compliance, a mobile notary business needs clients. This section focuses on the *initial steps* to establish your brand and attract your first clients, building visibility from the ground up.

Establish Your Core Online Presence:

- **Professional Website (Basic):** Start with a simple, mobile-friendly website. This is your digital storefront. Focus on clear service descriptions, your defined service area, transparent pricing, and prominent contact information. As I learned, "The excitement ensued. The following are the steps to getting through the beginning steps for us." (from *Quick & Easy Solutions*). Your website is where clients will first learn about you.

- **Google My Business (GMB) Profile:** This is paramount for local discoverability. Claim and fully optimize your GMB listing with accurate business information, services, hours, and photos. Encourage initial client reviews. As I noted in *Quick & Easy Solutions*, "We started with only filling in the basics. As time went on, we looked at other local companies and needed to strengthen our SEO for our Business page." This is a continuous effort.
- **Professional Email:** Use a professional email address (e.g., `yourname@yourbusinessname.com`) for all business communications. As I mentioned in *Quick & Easy Solutions*, "It looks professional and easy to associate with the business name. This does come with a monthly cost. It makes for great branding."

Basic Marketing Materials:

- **Professional Business Cards:** Design and print high-quality business cards with your business name, contact information, website, and a clear statement of services (e.g., "Mobile Notary Public"). These are essential for networking and leaving a professional impression.
- **Initial Networking:** Begin connecting with potential referral sources in your local area (e.g., local real estate agents, small law firms, senior centers) to introduce your services. Personal connections are powerful.

Conclusion

Establishing a successful mobile notary business is a strategic endeavor that extends far beyond simply obtaining a notary commission. It requires diligent planning in business structure, meticulous attention to insurance and legal compliance, and thoughtful initial investments in essential equipment to create a truly functional mobile office. By systematically addressing each of these foundational components—from choosing your legal entity and securing necessary registrations to setting up your initial equipment and launching your core marketing efforts—you can build a robust, compliant, and professional mobile notary business. This solid groundwork, combined with effective initial marketing, sets the stage for long-term growth, profitability, and a stellar reputation in the marketplace, ensuring you are prepared to confidently deliver exceptional service from day one.

Chapter 3: Equipping Your Mobile Office: Essential Tools for On-the-Go Excellence

Welcome back to "The Mobile Notary Blueprint." In Chapter 1, I shared my personal journey into the mobile notary revolution, highlighting the immense advantages of offering on-demand services. Following that, in Chapter 2, we meticulously laid the crucial legal and financial groundwork for your business, ensuring you're building on a solid, protected foundation. Now, it's time to talk about the very physical manifestation of your mobile notary enterprise: **equipping your mobile office**. In my years with Mobile Notary by Derrick Spruill, I've learned that having precisely the right tools and supplies isn't just about convenience; it's absolutely essential for ensuring strict compliance with complex state laws, performing notarial acts with unwavering accuracy and precision, maintaining a consistently high level of professionalism in every client interaction, significantly enhancing your operational efficiency, and, crucially, protecting you from potential liability and fraudulent schemes. Your notary bag isn't just a bag; it's your portable command center, and every item within it plays a vital, interconnected role in your daily success.

I. Introduction: Your Notary Bag as Your Portable Command Center

When I first started out as a mobile notary, I quickly realized that my ability to serve clients effectively and reliably on-demand depended entirely on my preparedness. I couldn't afford the embarrassment or the professional setback of arriving at a signing missing a crucial stamp, a specific type of pen, or an effective way to verify an unfamiliar ID. My approach to equipment investment has always been strategic and deliberate: every tool must directly contribute to efficiency, compliance, and professionalism. This section focuses on the initial, foundational investments that will transform your vehicle and your notary bag into a fully functional, secure, and professional mobile office, ready to handle diverse client needs seamlessly on the go, no matter the location or time. It's about building a system that gives you confidence and minimizes surprises.

I vividly recall an instance early in my career where I was called for a last-minute signing, a seemingly straightforward acknowledgment. I arrived promptly, only to realize with a sinking feeling that I had grabbed the wrong notary stamp from my office, one that was nearly out of ink. The impression it produced was faint, barely legible, and certainly not up to my standards of operational excellence (as I detail in *Notary Operational Excellence*). I had to apologize profusely to the client, reschedule the appointment, and return later with a fresh, fully inked stamp. That single incident, while seemingly minor, taught me the profound and immediate impact of preparedness. It wasn't just an inconvenience; it was a direct hit to my burgeoning professionalism, a waste of everyone's valuable time, and a moment of unnecessary stress. From that day forward, I vowed to always be meticulously over-prepared, a principle I now diligently share with you, ensuring that such a scenario never compromises your service or reputation.

II. Core Notary Essentials: Non-Negotiable for Every Act

These are the absolute must-have items that every Notary Public, especially one operating as a mobile notary, must possess and have readily available and in perfect working order for every single notarial act. Without these fundamental instruments, you cannot legally or properly perform your duties, and attempting to do so will lead to severe misconduct, invalid notarizations, and significant legal and financial ramifications. These items are the fundamental instruments of your public office and represent your legal authority, acting as extensions of your commission.

Official Notary Seal/Stamp:

- **Purpose:** Your official, state-compliant notary seal is your unique, legally recognized mark of authority. It is legally required by virtually all states to authenticate your notarial acts on paper documents. The seal contains specific information mandated by your state, such as your name (exactly as commissioned), the words "Notary Public," your state of commission, and usually your commission number and expiration date.
- **Importance:** The seal provides tangible, visual proof that the notarial act was performed by a duly commissioned notary. A clear, legible, and complete impression is absolutely crucial for the document's acceptance by receiving parties (e.g., county recorders, banks, courts, government agencies). An illegible, smudged, partial, or incomplete seal impression can lead to immediate document rejection, causing significant delays, additional costs for the client, and potential liability for you. It also serves as a critical anti-fraud feature, as legitimate seals are designed with intricate details that are difficult to counterfeit accurately. The distinct impression helps verify the document's authenticity at a glance.
- **Best Practice:** Ensure your stamp is always clean and produces a clear, crisp impression in the approved ink color (refer to Chapter 3 of *Notary Operational Excellence* for specific state requirements, typically dark blue or black, permanent ink). Carry a fresh, adequately inked pad if using a self-inking stamp (as ink can dry out), or a separate, well-inked stamp pad for traditional rubber stamps. I personally carry multiple types of stamps—small circle, rectangular self-inking, and even an embosser stamp—to accommodate

different document spaces and client preferences, as detailed in my book *Quick & Easy Solutions*. Consider carrying a backup stamp if permitted by your state's laws, or know where to quickly obtain a replacement, as a damaged, lost, or malfunctioning seal can immediately halt your operations and prevent you from performing notarizations, causing lost revenue and client frustration.

Notary Journal:

- **Purpose:** Your bound, tamper-evident notary journal is the chronological, legally mandated record of every single notarial act you perform. It documents all the essential details of each notarization.
- **Importance:** It is mandatory in the vast majority of states (and universally considered a paramount best practice even where optional). The journal serves as your primary defense in lawsuits and complaints, providing an irrefutable audit trail of your diligence and compliance. It is a powerful tool for fraud prevention, as fraudsters are often deterred by the knowledge that their identity and actions will be permanently recorded in an official, tamper-evident log. It also serves as an undeniable testament to your compliance with state laws and an invaluable memory aid for recalling specific transaction details years later.

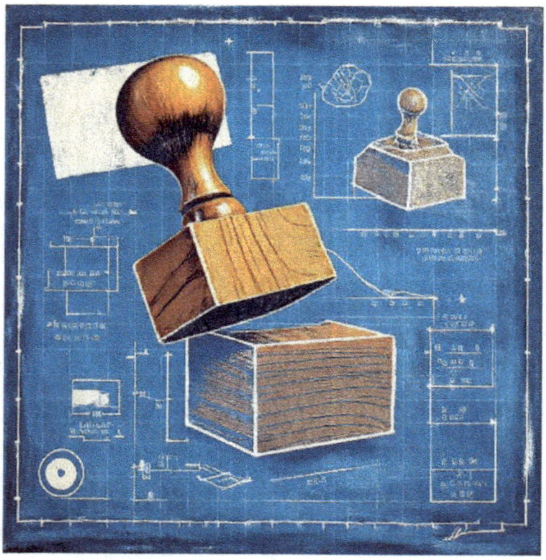

- **Best Practice:** Always have your current notary journal with you and ensure it is securely stored and protected from unauthorized access, damage (e.g., water, fire, extreme temperatures), or theft. Verify that it complies with your state's specific requirements (e.g., pre-numbered pages, specific columns for required entries like signer's address, ID type, document title, fee, and often a mandatory thumbprint in states like California and Texas). (Refer to Chapter 2 of *Notary Operational Excellence* for detailed journaling requirements and best practices for secure storage and meticulous maintenance.)

High-Quality Pens (Approved Ink Colors):

- **Purpose:** For the signer's wet-ink signature, your official signature, and for accurately completing the notarial certificate and notary journal entries.
- **Importance:** Using the correct type and color of ink is critical for document integrity, legibility, and long-term preservation. State laws often specify ink color (refer to Chapter 3 of *Notary Operational Excellence* for specific requirements, typically dark blue or black). Poor quality, non-permanent, or dye-based inks can fade over time, smudge easily, or bleed through paper, compromising the document's integrity and potentially rendering the notarization invalid or illegible for archival purposes. The choice of ink directly impacts the longevity and legal acceptance of your work.
- **Best Practice:** Invest in a variety of high-quality, reliable pens that use archival-quality, pigment-based ink. These inks are specifically formulated to be waterproof, fade-resistant, and non-smearing, ensuring the longevity and integrity of your signatures and entries for decades. Always carry multiple pens in approved colors (blue and/or black) in case one runs out, is lost, malfunctions, or is misplaced during an appointment. As I advise in *Quick & Easy Solutions*, "Carry plenty of ink pens to the signing. Bring at least two black ink pens and at least two blue ink pens... There’s nothing more professional than having a backup plan and accommodating the client when the

needs arise." Having a variety of tip sizes (fine, medium) can also be helpful for different signing needs and document types.

Loose Notarial Certificates (All Types):

- **Purpose:** These are blank, pre-printed, state-compliant notary certificates for common notarial acts such as Acknowledgments, Jurats, and any other acts your state permits (e.g., Copy Certifications).
- **Importance:** Loose certificates are absolutely crucial for situations where the document presented by the client either lacks a pre-printed notarial certificate entirely, has incorrect or outdated wording that does not comply with current state law, or is missing a certificate on a particular page. In such cases, you can then attach the correct, compliant loose certificate securely to the document, ensuring the notarization meets all legal requirements. Never alter pre-printed wording on a document; always attach a correct loose certificate if the existing one is unusable, as altering a document can lead to severe penalties.
- **Best Practice:** Maintain a sufficient supply of each type of certificate you commonly perform. Ensure they are compliant with your state's current wording and are securely organized and protected from damage in your notary bag. Familiarize yourself with your state's rules for attaching loose certificates (e.g., stapling location, required linking statements) to prevent them from being detached and fraudulently affixed to another document.

State-Specific Notary Handbook/Guidelines (Physical or Digital):

- **Purpose:** Your state's official notary handbook or a comprehensive quick reference guide containing all relevant notary laws, rules, and procedures.
- **Importance:** Even if you've memorized a significant portion of your state's notary law, having the physical handbook or a readily accessible digital version (e.g., on your tablet/laptop) is invaluable. It serves as your ultimate legal reference for

looking up specific rules on the spot, especially for unusual situations, complex document types, or when you need to confirm a precise legal detail (e.g., acceptable ID for a specific scenario, proper wording for a unique certificate, or a specific prohibited act). This ensures unwavering accuracy, compliance, and serves as a powerful defense in case of questions or disputes. It demonstrates your commitment to being a knowledgeable authority.
- **Best Practice:** Keep a physical copy in your notary bag or a digital version readily accessible on your mobile devices. Ensure it's the most current edition, as notary laws can change frequently due to new legislative sessions or administrative updates.

III. Identity Verification Aids: Enhancing Your Fraud Shield

As I emphasized in *Notary Fraud Shield*, your role as a fraud shield begins with rigorous identity verification. These specialized tools significantly enhance your ability to meticulously verify a signer's identity, providing a critical and multi-layered defense against impersonation and document fraud. They allow you to go beyond a simple visual check and scrutinize identification documents for subtle signs of authenticity or tampering, adding layers of security that deter sophisticated fraudsters.

Magnifying Glass:

- **Purpose:** For scrutinizing tiny details on identification documents that are not visible to the naked eye.
- **Importance:** Absolutely essential for examining micro-printing (extremely tiny text visible only under magnification, a common security feature on modern IDs), fine lines, intricate patterns, and other small security features embedded in identification documents. It also helps detect subtle alterations, erasures, or signs of tampering (e.g., blurred lines,

altered fonts, evidence of layers, or inconsistencies in the printing) that might indicate a fraudulent ID.

- **Best Practice:** A small, portable jeweler's loupe (with 10x or 30x magnification) or a compact magnifying glass with a built-in LED light is ideal for clear visibility in various lighting conditions, ensuring you can thoroughly inspect the ID's details and security elements.

UV Light (Ultraviolet Light):

- **Purpose:** For checking ultraviolet (UV) security features present on many modern identification documents and currency.
- **Importance:** Many contemporary driver's licenses, state ID cards, and passports incorporate security features (e.g., hidden images, patterns, text, or ghost images) that are only visible under ultraviolet light. These features are extremely difficult for counterfeiters to replicate accurately. A UV light is a powerful and relatively inexpensive tool for detecting counterfeit IDs that might otherwise appear genuine under normal lighting conditions. It's a quick, effective, and often surprising way to add a layer of verification that fraudsters may not anticipate.
- **Best Practice:** A small, portable UV flashlight (often available for under $20) is highly effective and a crucial addition to your ID verification toolkit. Ensure it has sufficient wattage to illuminate the UV features clearly and that you know what to look for on common IDs in your state.

ID Card Reader (Optional, but for Advanced Verification):

- **Purpose:** Electronically reads and verifies data from the magnetic stripe, barcode, or embedded chip on certain identification documents.
- **Importance:** Provides an enhanced, automated layer of verification by cross-referencing information printed on the physical ID with data stored digitally. This can quickly flag inconsistencies, expired IDs, or invalid IDs that might not be

apparent through visual inspection alone. This tool is particularly useful for high-volume notaries, those performing Remote Online Notarization (RON) where digital credential analysis is a core component, or notaries working with corporate clients who require enhanced security protocols. It adds a technological layer of trust.

- **Best Practice:** Research state-approved devices and software if considering this, especially for RON, as specific technology requirements apply. This is a more significant investment but offers advanced security capabilities and can streamline the ID verification process, providing a documented digital record of the ID check.

IV. Mobile Office Technology: Powering Your On-Demand Operations

For a mobile notary, technology is not just a convenience; it's the indispensable engine that drives efficiency, expands service capabilities, and significantly enhances professionalism. These are crucial initial investments to consider for your mobile operations, enabling you to deliver seamless, modern service.

Reliable Laptop or Tablet:

- **Purpose:** A portable computing device is absolutely essential for managing virtually every aspect of your mobile notary business.
- **Importance:** It allows you to access electronic documents (e.g., loan packages, contracts), manage your schedule and appointments efficiently, communicate with clients via email or messaging apps, and is fundamental if you plan to pursue Remote Online Notarization (RON) or Electronic Notarization (eNotary). A larger screen provides comfortable document review, enables the use of various business software (e.g., CRM, invoicing, scheduling apps), and is fundamental for interacting with RON platforms. It allows for efficient

digital workflows and comprehensive client management on the go.

- **Best Practice:** Choose a device that is lightweight for easy portability, has excellent battery life to last through multiple appointments, and is equipped with necessary cybersecurity software (antivirus, firewall, VPN) to protect sensitive client data and maintain confidentiality, especially when connecting to public Wi-Fi networks.

Mobile Hotspot / Reliable Internet Access:

- **Purpose:** Provides a consistent, secure, and portable internet connection for your laptop/tablet and other devices while you are on the go, independent of client Wi-Fi.
- **Importance:** Crucial for accessing cloud-based documents, checking urgent emails, managing online booking systems, and absolutely critical for conducting RON sessions, which demand a stable, high-speed, and secure internet connection for clear audio-visual quality, seamless identity verification processes, and reliable document transfer. Unreliable internet can halt a signing mid-process, leading to frustration, delays, and lost business.
- **Best Practice:** A dedicated mobile hotspot device or a smartphone with a robust data plan and reliable hotspot capability is highly recommended. Consider a backup internet option (e.g., a secondary carrier's hotspot) if you operate in areas with spotty coverage or for mission-critical digital notarizations.

Portable Printer/Scanner:

- **Purpose:** A compact, lightweight, and often battery-powered portable printer/scanner.
- **Importance:** An invaluable asset, especially for Loan Signing Agents (LSAs) who frequently deal with voluminous document packages. It allows you to print last-minute documents (e.g., a forgotten page, extra copies of disclosures), print entire loan packages on-site (saving significant time, gas,

and the need for a separate trip to a print shop), or scan signed documents back to clients or title companies immediately from the field. This significantly enhances client convenience, streamlines workflows, and reduces delays. As I mentioned in *Quick & Easy Solutions*, having a printer allows you to offer the value-added service of printing documents for a fee, and "This system saves time when the client needs information immediately when you're not at your computer."

- **Best Practice:** Choose a model known for its reliability, good battery life, high print quality (especially for legal documents), and ease of connectivity (e.g., Bluetooth, Wi-Fi). For LSAs, a high-speed laser printer with dual-tray capability for legal and letter-sized paper is often a necessary, albeit larger, investment.

GPS/Navigation Device:

- **Purpose:** For optimal route planning and accurate navigation to client locations.
- **Importance:** Essential for efficient travel, avoiding traffic congestion, finding client locations quickly, and providing accurate estimated arrival times (ETAs). This reduces stress, saves valuable time and fuel costs, and ensures unwavering punctuality, which is a hallmark of professional mobile notary service. Getting lost or arriving late due to poor navigation undermines professionalism.

- **Best Practice:** Use reliable, up-to-date navigation apps (e.g., Google Maps, Waze, Apple Maps) that offer real-time traffic updates, multi-stop optimization, and clear, voice-guided directions. Keep your maps updated and consider offline map capabilities for areas with poor cell service.

V. Organizational & Convenience Supplies: Staying Prepared

Beyond the core notary tools and technology, a well-stocked and meticulously organized notary bag with various convenience supplies ensures you're prepared for any situation, can handle unexpected client needs, and maintain professionalism on the go. These are the small details that make a big difference in operational excellence.

Professional Briefcase/Notary Bag:

- **Purpose:** A sturdy, organized, and professional-looking briefcase or notary bag for safely and securely carrying all your supplies and documents.
- **Importance:** Keeps documents and supplies organized, protected from damage (e.g., spills, bending, tearing), and easily accessible during appointments. It also presents a professional image to clients, signaling organization and preparedness. It should allow for easy access to frequently used items while keeping sensitive documents and notary tools securely separated and protected. As I've experienced, using a "pluck foam case" for notary supplies ensures "everything is easy to find and stays put. When we pack up to leave, we can quickly identify any items left behind before leaving the signing." (from *Quick & Easy Solutions*). This prevents lost items and maintains efficiency.
- **Best Practice:** Choose a durable, water-resistant bag with multiple compartments, secure zippers (ideally lockable for sensitive items like your journal), and comfortable carrying straps.

Essential Organizational Supplies:

- **Paper Clips/Binder Clips:** Essential for organizing multi-page documents and keeping related papers together without stapling prematurely, especially for loan packages where documents need to be separated for recording or specific processing.
- **Stapler and Staple Remover:** A reliable, heavy-duty stapler is crucial for securely attaching loose notarial certificates to documents and for organizing multi-page documents. A staple remover helps correct stapling errors without damaging the document.
- **Small Flashlight:** Useful for dimly lit environments (e.g., a client's dimly lit home, a poorly lit hallway, or checking a car's interior for documents) or for scrutinizing security features on IDs in less-than-ideal lighting conditions.
- **Clipboard/Portable Writing Surface:** Provides a firm, stable surface for signers to write on, especially if a table is unavailable or uncomfortable. This is particularly helpful for elderly clients signing in bed, as I've found, ensuring a smooth and comfortable signing experience.
- **Sticky Notes/Flags:** For marking pages for signatures or initials, or for leaving temporary notes for the client or yourself.
- **Document Folders/Envelopes:** For separating and protecting signed originals, borrower copies, and documents to be returned to the hiring entity. This prevents mixing up documents and ensures secure transport of sensitive information.
- **Postal Service Envelopes:** As I advise in *Quick & Easy Solutions*, keeping "one or two of each readily available for every visit" allows you to offer an "additional service when a client wants the notarized document mailed immediately after the signing appointment." This is a simple value-add that can impress clients.

VI. Payment Processing Tools: Ensuring Seamless Transactions

Efficient and flexible payment processing is vital for a mobile notary business, ensuring you get paid promptly and professionally, and offering maximum convenience to your clients. Streamlined payment options enhance the overall client experience and improve your business's cash flow.

Mobile Card Reader:

- **Purpose:** Devices like Square, PayPal Here, or Stripe Terminal connect wirelessly to your smartphone or tablet, allowing you to accept credit/debit card payments on the spot.
- **Importance:** Offers immense convenience to clients who may not carry cash or checks. This significantly increases your payment options, improves your cash flow by enabling immediate payment, and eliminates the hassle of invoicing for smaller jobs. Many clients prefer the ease and security of card payments. As I noted in *Quick & Easy Solutions*, "We have enjoyed such great benefits from using Square over the years. Easy to use by tap, dip, or swipe. Recently, we can now use the tap feature with the RF or RFID or radio frequency contactless credit card software without the hardware directly on our phone." This ease of payment is a significant customer service advantage that sets you apart.
- **Best Practice:** Choose a reader with competitive transaction fees, a reliable mobile app, and good customer support. Ensure you understand the fees associated with each transaction and how they impact your profitability.

Invoicing App/Software:

- **Purpose:** For creating and sending professional, itemized invoices to clients.
- **Importance:** Essential for corporate clients, title companies, or when offering specialized services that require detailed billing and payment tracking. Helps manage accounts

receivable, provides a professional billing record, and simplifies accounting for your business. Many apps also allow for online payment directly from the invoice, further streamlining the payment process.

- **Best Practice:** Use a reputable invoicing software that integrates with your accounting system (if applicable) for seamless financial management and accurate record-keeping.

Receipt Book:

- **Purpose:** For providing physical, handwritten receipts for cash payments.
- **Importance:** Ensures transparency and provides a clear record for both you and the client, simplifying their expense tracking or reimbursement processes. Always provide a receipt for every payment received, regardless of method, as this is a mark of professionalism and accountability.

Conclusion

Equipping yourself with precisely the right tools and supplies is a critical and ongoing investment in the success, compliance, and professionalism of your mobile notary business. From core notary essentials like your official seal and journal to advanced identity verification aids, a fully functional mobile office setup, and robust payment processing tools, each item plays a vital role in ensuring accurate notarial acts, maximizing efficiency, enhancing client satisfaction, and protecting you from liability. By meticulously organizing and maintaining these essential tools, and by prioritizing personal safety and unwavering professional conduct, Notaries Public can confidently deliver exceptional service, uphold their public trust, and thrive in the dynamic and rewarding world of mobile notarization, building a reputation for reliability, expertise, and excellence that sets them apart in the marketplace. Your preparedness is not just a convenience; it is your competitive edge and a cornerstone of your professional integrity.

Chapter 4: Pricing for Profit: Structuring Your Fees Strategically

In the previous chapters of "The Mobile Notary Blueprint," we've established the compelling reasons to embrace mobile notary work (Chapter 1) and meticulously built the legal and financial foundations for your business (Chapter 2) and equipped your mobile office (Chapter 3). Now, it's time to tackle one of the most vital, and often perplexing, aspects of running a successful mobile notary business: **pricing for profit**. This isn't just about picking a number; it's about strategically structuring your fees to reflect the immense value you provide, ensure compliance, and guarantee your business's long-term financial health. As I've learned through Mobile Notary by Derrick Spruill and discussed on my "Notary Knowledge by Derrick Spruill" podcast, getting your pricing right is absolutely fundamental to your success and sustainability.

I. Introduction: Value, Transparency, and Profitability – The Pricing Equation

When I first transitioned from my corporate career to full-time mobile notary work, one of the biggest questions on my whiteboard was, "What prices do I charge?" It's a question every notary entrepreneur grapples with. My philosophy has always been centered on a clear equation: **Value + Transparency = Profitability**. You deliver immense value through convenience and expertise. Your pricing must be transparent to build trust. And ultimately, your fees must ensure your business is profitable and sustainable.

Why Strategic Pricing is Key to Mobile Notary Success: Strategic pricing is far more than just covering costs; it's the engine of your mobile notary business. It directly impacts:

- **Your Income:** Fair pricing ensures you are adequately compensated for your time, expertise, and mobility.

- **Client Perception:** Transparent and consistent pricing builds trust and professionalism. Clients appreciate knowing what to expect.
- **Competitiveness:** Your pricing needs to be competitive within your local market, but also reflect your unique value proposition.
- **Sustainability:** Your fees must cover all your operational costs (fuel, supplies, insurance, technology) and provide a profit margin for growth.
- **Work-Life Balance:** As I often ask, "What is your number? I mean, what are you worth? What do you need to manage your finances versus your private time?" (from *Quick & Easy Solutions: How to Increase Mobile Notary Business for More Success & Profit*). Strategic pricing allows you to earn enough to make the effort worthwhile, even after a long day.

My Philosophy on Fair and Competitive Fees: My philosophy is to set prices that are fair to the client, competitive within my service area (Loudoun, Fairfax, and Prince William Counties in Virginia), and, crucially, that adequately compensate me for my time and effort. I believe in being straightforward and simple with pricing, removing all doubt for the customer. This approach has proven successful for Mobile Notary by Derrick Spruill, contributing to consistent customer growth and revenue increases.

II. Understanding Notary Act Fees: State-Regulated Charges

The core of a notary's income, and the most fundamental component of their pricing structure, comes directly from performing official notarial acts. These fees are almost universally regulated by state law, meaning there is a strict, legally mandated maximum amount you can charge per signature or per act. This regulation is primarily in place to protect the public from excessive or exploitative charges for what is considered a public service.

Per Signature/Per Act Maximums (Strictly Regulated by State Law):

- **State-Specific Caps and Their Rationale:** Every state sets a maximum fee that a Notary Public can charge for each individual notarial act performed. This statutory maximum typically ranges from a relatively low of $2 (in some states, reflecting older statutes) to a higher cap of $15 or $25 per signature or per act in others. This fee represents the state's determination of a fair charge for the notary's official act itself. It is a legal ceiling; you cannot, under any circumstances, charge more than this maximum. However, you are always permitted to charge less than the maximum fee, or even perform acts for free (though performing acts for free is generally not advisable for a business seeking profitability and can sometimes be viewed as compromising impartiality if not handled carefully). The rationale behind these caps is rooted in the notary's status as a public official, ensuring that essential authentication services remain accessible and affordable to the general populace, while also preventing price gouging. Variations in caps often reflect differences in state legislative priorities, cost of living, and historical precedents.
- **Examples of Common State Caps (Illustrative, always verify current law):** These examples demonstrate the range of statutory fees. It is imperative that you consult your specific state's current notary handbook for the exact figures.
    - **California:** $15 per signature for an Acknowledgment or Jurat. This is one of the higher per-signature fees and serves as a common benchmark for many notaries, especially those considering mobile services.
    - **Florida:** $10 per signature/act.
    - **Texas:** $6 for the first signature, and $1 for each additional signature for an Acknowledgment; $6 for a Jurat. Texas has a more granular and often lower per-signature fee structure compared to some other states.
    - **Virginia:** $10 per signature/act.
- **Severe Consequences of Overcharging:** It is a serious violation of notary law to charge more than your state's

maximum allowable fee for a notarial act. This is not a minor infraction. Doing so can lead to severe administrative penalties imposed by your commissioning authority, including substantial administrative fines (which can range from hundreds to thousands of dollars per violation), temporary suspension of your notary commission, or even permanent revocation of your notary commission. Beyond administrative action, overcharging can also lead to civil lawsuits from aggrieved clients seeking to recover the overcharged amount and potentially additional damages. This is why meticulous adherence to these caps is absolutely non-negotiable and must be a core principle of your pricing strategy.

- **Thorough State-Specific Research is Non-Negotiable:** It is absolutely essential and your primary, ongoing responsibility to know your state's *current* maximum allowable fees for *each specific type* of notarial act (Acknowledgment, Jurat, Oath/Affirmation, Copy Certification, Witnessing a Signature, etc.). This information is always found in your state's official notary handbook, on the Secretary of State's official website, or through reputable state notary associations. Do not rely on information from other states, general online sources, or anecdotal evidence. Laws can change, so regular verification is critical.

What Constitutes a "Notarial Act" for Fee Purposes: Clarity in Billing: Understanding precisely what constitutes a "notarial act" for which you can charge a fee is key to accurate billing and avoiding disputes.

- **Per Signature:** For common notarial acts like Acknowledgments and Jurats, the fee is typically charged per signature notarized. If a document has two signers, and each signer requires an acknowledgment of their signature, that constitutes two distinct notarial acts, and you can charge your state's maximum fee for each. Similarly, if one signer signs a document multiple times, and each signature requires a separate notarial certificate (e.g., signing both as an individual and as a corporate officer), each distinct notarization is chargeable.

- **Per Oath/Affirmation:** For simple oaths or affirmations administered without an accompanying signature on a document (e.g., swearing in a witness for a deposition, or administering an oath for a sworn statement where the signer does not sign in your presence), the fee is usually charged per oath administered.
- **Per Copy Certified:** If your state's laws permit you to perform copy certifications (as discussed in Chapter 4 of *Notary Operational Excellence*), the fee is typically charged per copy certified, not per page of the copy. For example, if a client needs a 5-page document copy-certified, and your state allows $10 per copy, you charge $10, not $50.
- **Journal Entry:** The act of making a journal entry is an integral and mandatory part of performing the notarial act itself and is therefore not a separate chargeable fee. The statutory fee for the notarial act covers the entire notarial process, including the journal entry, ID verification, and certificate completion.
- **Non-Chargeable Activities:** You cannot charge a separate fee for activities that are part of your basic duty or are not defined as a notarial act. This includes:
    - Answering general questions about your services.
    - Reviewing identification (this is part of the notarial act).
    - Assessing willingness and awareness (also part of the act).
    - Explaining your fees.
    - Waiting for a client *within* an agreed-upon grace period (though waiting fees *after* a grace period are common, as discussed below).

III. Travel Fees: Compensating for Convenience and Mobility

This is the primary and most significant area where mobile notaries differentiate themselves financially from traditional in-office notaries and generate substantial additional income. Travel fees compensate the notary for their valuable time, mileage, and vehicle expenses incurred traveling to and from the client's location, thereby providing unparalleled convenience. Unlike notary act fees, travel fees are generally *not* regulated by state law (though some states may have specific disclosure requirements or general guidelines, and all fees must be reasonable).

Compensation for Time and Mileage: The True Cost of Mobility:

- **Beyond the Signature:** The travel fee is meticulously designed to cover your direct operational costs and, crucially, your unproductive time. This includes:
    - **Fuel Costs:** The direct expense of gasoline or other fuel for your vehicle.
    - **Vehicle Wear and Tear:** Costs associated with vehicle maintenance, repairs, and depreciation due to extensive mileage.
    - **Notary's Non-Billable Time:** This is often the largest component. It covers time spent driving to the client's location, navigating unfamiliar routes, searching for parking, waiting for the client to arrive or prepare documents, and packing/unpacking supplies. This time is not billable as a notarial act, but it is absolutely essential to providing the mobile service and must be compensated.

  - **Opportunity Cost:** The travel time also represents an opportunity cost—time that could have been spent on another billable notarization or other income-generating activities.
- **Negotiable and Market-Driven:** Since these fees are generally unregulated by state law, you have the significant flexibility to set your travel fees based on your actual business costs, the competitive rates in your specific service area, and the perceived value of the convenience you provide. Researching what other mobile notaries in your region charge for comparable distances and services is a good starting point for establishing competitive yet profitable rates.

Structuring Travel Fees (Common Models for Clarity and Predictability): Choosing a clear, predictable, and easily understandable structure for your travel fees is paramount. It enhances transparency for clients and simplifies your quoting process.

- **Flat Fee:** This is a single, fixed fee charged for travel within a certain predefined geographical radius from your base location (e.g., "$50 for travel up to 10 miles from my home office"). This model is straightforward for both the notary to quote and the client to understand, making it very popular. It works well for consistent local travel within your primary service zone.
  - *Pros:* Simplicity, easy quoting, predictable for client.
  - *Cons:* May not perfectly capture costs for varied distances within the flat fee zone.
- **Tiered Fee:** This model involves increasing fees based on concentric mileage tiers from your base location (e.g., "$50 for 0-10 miles, $75 for 11-20 miles, $100 for 21-30 miles, and so on"). This structure more fairly accounts for increased travel time and costs as distance increases, providing a clear and justifiable progression for clients.
  - *Pros:* Fairer cost distribution based on distance, clear progression.
  - *Cons:* Slightly more complex to quote initially, requires a mileage calculator.

- **Mileage-Based:** Charging a specific per-mile rate (e.g., "$0.75 per mile round trip") from your base location to the client's location. This is the most precise method for covering actual mileage costs.
  - *Pros:* Most accurate reflection of mileage costs, highly justifiable.
  - *Cons:* Can be more complex to quote quickly without a precise mileage calculation tool, may result in uneven total fees.
- **Time-Based:** Charging an hourly rate specifically for travel time (e.g., "$60 per hour for travel time, billed in 15-minute increments"). This method is less common for general mobile notary services but might be used for specialized, unpredictable assignments or for very long distances where travel time is the dominant cost factor, especially if traffic is unpredictable.
  - *Pros:* Accounts for traffic and variable travel times.
  - *Cons:* Less predictable for the client upfront, can be harder to estimate.

Absolute Transparency and Upfront Communication: The Cornerstone of Trust:

- **Crucial for Client Satisfaction and Trust:** Always, without exception, clearly and explicitly communicate your travel fee *before* the appointment is confirmed and before you begin travel. This is absolutely paramount for managing client expectations, preventing misunderstandings, and ensuring high client satisfaction. Surprising a client with a travel fee at the time of service is a primary cause of negative reviews, client disputes, and complaints to your commissioning authority.
- **Written Quote/Fee Schedule:** Provide a written quote or a clear, accessible fee schedule. This can be done via your website, a detailed email, or a text message. A written record provides a tangible reference for both you and the client, minimizing ambiguity.

- **Separate from Notary Act Fee:** Clearly and repeatedly state that the travel fee is separate from, and in addition to, the per-signature notary act fees. This helps clients understand why they are paying more than the state-mandated maximum for a single signature and avoids any confusion about state-mandated caps on notarial acts. For example, a clear quote might be: "My fee for notarizing your document is $15 per signature, plus a travel fee of $50, for a total of $65 for one signature."

IV. Specialized Service Fees: Beyond Basic Notarization (Unlocking Higher Value)

Many mobile notaries strategically choose to offer specialized services that command significantly higher, often flat-rate, fees. These premiums are entirely justified by the increased complexity, greater time commitment, specialized knowledge, investment in specific training and equipment, and often higher liability associated with these advanced offerings.

Loan Signing Agent (LSA) Fees:

- **Specialization:** LSAs are notaries who have received additional, in-depth training and often certification (e.g., through the National Notary Association's Notary Signing Agent (NSA) program) to specialize in guiding borrowers through the complex and voluminous packages of real estate loan documents (e.g., mortgages, refinances, home equity lines of credit - HELOCs, reverse mortgages, and various other security instruments).
- **Fee Structure:** LSA fees are typically structured as flat fees, ranging significantly (e.g., from $75 to $200+ per signing, and sometimes much higher for complex or last-minute closings, or for specific document types like reverse mortgages, depending on location, complexity, and volume of documents). This comprehensive flat fee usually covers:
    - Travel to the client's location.

    - All notarizations required within the typically large loan package (often 10-20+ notarized signatures).
    - Printing the often voluminous loan documents (sometimes 100-200+ pages, requiring significant paper and toner costs).
    - A thorough pre-review of the entire package for completeness and accuracy before the signing.
    - Expertly guiding the borrower through the signing process, identifying each document and its purpose (without giving legal advice).
    - Meticulous post-signing review to ensure all signatures, initials, and dates are correctly placed.
    - Proper packaging and often courier services (e.g., FedEx, UPS) for timely return of documents to the title company or lender.
- **Why Higher Fees are Justified:** The higher fees for LSAs are fully justified because they compensate for the specialized training and knowledge required, the significant time commitment (often 1-2 hours per signing, plus printing and travel), the high document volume, substantial printing costs, the critical and time-sensitive nature of these transactions (delays can cost thousands in missed rate locks or penalties), and the heightened liability associated with high-value real estate documents.

Apostille and Authentication Services:

- **Purpose:** Notaries often facilitate the authentication of U.S. documents for international use. This involves an initial notarization of the document (if it's a private document), followed by obtaining an "apostille" (a single certificate for countries party to the Hague Apostille Convention) or managing a complex, multi-step "authentication" process (for non-Hague Convention countries, involving state, federal, and potentially embassy/consulate offices). This service is crucial for documents like diplomas for foreign study, birth certificates for international adoption, or business contracts for overseas ventures.

- **Fee Structure:** This is a separate, often substantial, service fee that compensates the notary for their concierge role. It covers:
    - Your time and specialized expertise in consulting with the client, reviewing the document for eligibility, and preparing it for authentication.
    - Travel time and mileage to the Secretary of State's office (and potentially county clerk, federal Department of State office in Washington D.C., or foreign embassy/consulate).
    - Significant waiting time at various government offices, which can be unpredictable.
    - Handling all submission procedures, tracking the document's progress, and retrieval of the authenticated document.
    - Administrative overhead (phone calls, emails, tracking, record-keeping).
    - Courier/shipping costs (which can be passed through directly to the client or included in a flat fee).
- **Distinction:** This facilitation fee is entirely distinct from the basic notary act fee for the underlying document (if you notarized it). It's a high-value concierge service that requires specific, in-depth knowledge of international document legalization processes and often involves navigating complex bureaucratic procedures.

Witness Provided Fee:

- **Scenario:** Some legal documents (e.g., certain wills, specific types of deeds, or medical directives) require the signatures of additional disinterested witnesses in addition to the notary's act. Clients may not have these witnesses readily available, especially for urgent or sensitive signings.
- **Fee Structure:** If you arrange for and provide additional disinterested witnesses (individuals who are not involved in the transaction and have no beneficial interest in the document), you can charge a separate fee for this service (e.g., $25 - $75 per witness). This fee is in addition to your notary

act fee and travel fees, compensating you for the time and effort of coordinating, securing, and ensuring the impartiality of these reliable witnesses.

I-9 Verification:

- **Purpose:** Notaries often act as authorized representatives for employers to complete Section 2 of the Form I-9, Employment Eligibility Verification. This involves physically examining a new employee's original identity and employment authorization documents on behalf of a remote employer.
- **Fee Structure:** You can charge a separate service fee for reviewing and completing Section 2 of the I-9 form. It is crucial to remember that this is a **non-notarial act** (as discussed in Chapter 22 of *Notary Knowledge: Reference Guide & Notary Bible*), so it is *not* subject to notary act fee caps. The fee compensates you for your time, travel, and expertise in I-9 compliance, which is highly valued by employers with remote workforces.

Ancillary Fees (Chargeable if Clearly Communicated and Justified): These are additional, smaller fees that can add up and should always be transparently communicated to the client upfront to avoid any surprises or disputes.

- **Printing/Scanning Fees:** You can charge per page for printing documents provided by the client (e.g., $0.10 - $0.25 per page for standard letter/legal paper, higher for color, specialized paper, or large volumes). You can also charge for scanning signed documents back to them (e.g., $1 per page, or a flat fee per document). This compensates for paper, ink, and equipment wear.
- **Waiting Fees:** If you are required to wait for a client beyond a predetermined grace period (e.g., 10-15 minutes from the scheduled appointment time), you can charge a waiting fee (e.g., $1 per minute, or a flat hourly rate after a certain time). This compensates you for unproductive time that could have

been spent on another signing. This policy should be clearly stated in your service agreement.

- **Cancellation/Rescheduling Fees:** Clearly define your policy for cancellations or reschedules, especially if done without sufficient notice (e.g., less than 2-4 hours before the appointment). A cancellation fee (e.g., a percentage of the travel fee or a flat amount) protects you from lost income due to last-minute changes.
- **After-Hours/Holiday Premiums:** For services performed outside your standard business hours (e.g., late evenings, early mornings, weekends) or on public holidays, you can charge a premium fee on top of your regular notary and travel rates. This compensates you for the inconvenience and the high demand for services during these non-traditional times.
- **Document Shipping/Courier Fees:** If you are required to ship documents via a courier service (e.g., FedEx, UPS) or a specialized legal courier, you can charge the actual shipping cost as a pass-through expense, plus a small handling fee for your time.

V. Payment Methods: Offering Client Flexibility

Efficient and flexible payment processing is vital for a mobile notary business, ensuring you get paid promptly and professionally, and offering maximum convenience to your clients. Streamlined payment options enhance the overall client experience and improve your business's cash flow.

Diverse Payment Options (Cash, Card, Digital Apps, Invoicing): Offering a variety of flexible payment methods accommodates client preferences and ensures prompt payment, reducing friction at the point of service. This typically includes:

- **Cash:** Always a simple option, but ensure you have change if needed.
- **Check:** Accept checks from reputable clients or businesses, but be aware of potential delays or bounced checks.
- **Credit/Debit Cards:** Accepting credit/debit cards via a mobile card reader (e.g., Square, PayPal Here, Stripe Terminal) connected wirelessly to your smartphone or tablet is highly recommended for professionalism and convenience. It significantly increases your payment options, improves your cash flow by enabling immediate payment, and eliminates the hassle of invoicing for smaller jobs. Many clients prefer the ease and security of card payments. As I noted in *Quick & Easy Solutions*, "We have enjoyed such great benefits from using Square over the years. Easy to use by tap, dip, or swipe. Recently, we can now use the tap feature with the RF or RFID or radio frequency contactless credit card software without the hardware directly on our phone." This ease of payment is a significant customer service advantage that sets you apart.
- **Digital Payment Apps:** Apps like Venmo, Cash App, or Zelle are increasingly popular for peer-to-peer payments and can be convenient for individual clients. For international transactions, services like KoronaPay might be relevant, as I've used.
- **Invoicing:** Especially for corporate clients, title companies, or ongoing business relationships, professional invoicing is standard practice. This allows for deferred payment and integrates with their accounting systems.

Importance of Providing Professional Receipts:

- Always provide a professional, itemized receipt for services rendered, detailing all charges (notary fees, travel fees, and any specialized service fees). This promotes transparency, is good business practice, and provides the client with a clear record for their own accounting or reimbursement. As I've learned, "We send a receipt by email once the bank checks are deposited." (from *Quick & Easy Solutions*). Accountability in billing is a mark of professionalism.

VI. Pricing Strategy and Competitiveness: Finding Your Sweet Spot

Setting the right prices for your mobile notary services is a dynamic and ongoing process that involves a strategic balance of your operational costs, the perceived value of your unique service proposition, and the competitive landscape in your local market. It's an iterative process of research, analysis, and adjustment to ensure both profitability and market appeal.

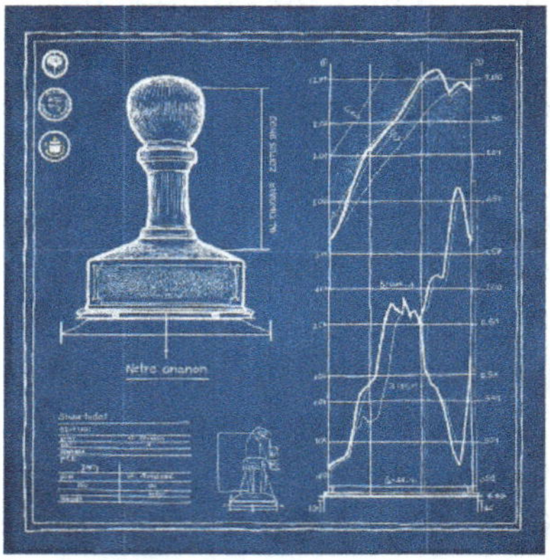

Calculate Your True Costs (Beyond Just Gas): Before setting any prices, meticulously calculate *all* your business costs. This includes not just obvious expenses like fuel and notary bond premiums, but also:

- **Direct Costs Per Signing:** Paper, toner, notary journal pages, pen ink, and any specific forms you provide.
- **Overhead Costs:** E&O insurance premiums, vehicle expenses (maintenance, depreciation, commercial auto insurance), website hosting, software subscriptions (e.g., RON platform, scheduling software, invoicing app), marketing

expenses, professional association dues, and continuing education costs.

- **Value of Your Time:** Assign an hourly rate to your time, including travel, waiting, and administrative tasks. Understanding your break-even point is essential to ensure profitability. As I often ask, "What is your number? I mean, what are you worth? What do you need to manage your finances versus your private time?" (from *Quick & Easy Solutions*). Your pricing should reflect your value.

Research Competitors and Understand Market Rates:

- Investigate what other mobile notaries in your specific service area are charging for similar services. This can involve checking their websites, Google My Business profiles, or even performing "mystery shopping" calls for quotes. You want to be competitive but avoid a "race to the bottom" that undervalues your services and makes profitability impossible. Identify the average market rate for each service type in your region.

Define and Emphasize Your Value Proposition (Why Choose You?):

- Clearly articulate what makes your mobile notary service unique, superior, or particularly valuable to clients. Is it unmatched speed for emergency signings, highly specialized expertise (e.g., complex trust signings, RON capabilities), unparalleled after-hours/weekend availability, a particular geographic focus (e.g., rural areas), or a consistently exceptional customer experience? Clients are often willing to pay a premium for convenience, reliability, and peace of mind. Your pricing should reflect this value.

Consider Tiered Services and Pricing Models:

- Instead of a simple, one-size-fits-all approach, consider offering different service tiers with corresponding pricing. For example:
    - **Standard Mobile Notary Service:** Your base rate for general notary work during business hours.
    - **Expedited/Emergency Mobile Notary Service:** A premium fee for immediate or short-notice appointments.
    - **Specialized Services:** Dedicated pricing for loan signings, apostille facilitation, or I-9 verifications. This allows you to cater to different client needs and price points, maximizing your revenue potential. As I noted in *Quick & Easy Solutions*, "We set our prices online. Every service has a fixed price. We offer traveling notary services. We offer loan signing agents. We offer an apostille service... We have prices for fingerprinting. We have a fixed price for Concierge Service and fees designated for document delivery services with the major delivery carriers."

Flexibility for Volume/Corporate Clients (Strategic Partnerships):

- For high-volume corporate clients, title companies, or ongoing business relationships, you may offer negotiated rates or volume discounts. While these rates might be lower per transaction, they provide consistent, predictable work volume. Ensure these negotiated rates are still profitable for your business after accounting for all costs.

Review and Adjust Regularly (Dynamic Pricing):

- The market for mobile notary services is dynamic. Periodically review your pricing strategy (e.g., quarterly or annually) to ensure it remains competitive, profitable, and aligned with your business goals. Adjust your fees as your operational costs change, as market demand shifts, as you gain more experience and specialized certifications, or as new competitors enter the market. Don't be afraid to raise your prices if your value justifies it. As I shared in *Quick & Easy Solutions*, "Once we initially set our prices, we did not change our prices. We are not the highest, and we are not the lowest. We found a sweet spot where we feel comfortable traveling to see a customer after working a long grueling day at our full-time job. The growth in our customer count has increased by 50% each year, and our revenue has increased by the same amount." This demonstrates the power of finding that "sweet spot."

Conclusion

Properly structuring and transparently communicating your pricing and fees are absolutely fundamental to the sustained success, long-term profitability, and ethical operation of a mobile notary business. By understanding the critical distinction between state-regulated notary act fees and negotiable travel and specialized service fees, you can create a clear, competitive, and highly profitable pricing model that accurately reflects the immense value you provide. Always prioritize transparent, upfront communication with clients to avoid misunderstandings, build unwavering trust, and ensure a positive customer experience that fosters loyalty and referrals. This meticulous approach to pricing not only reinforces your professionalism and compliance but also solidifies the indispensable value of your mobile notary services in today's demanding and evolving marketplace. Your fee structure is a direct reflection of your business acumen and commitment to integrity.

Chapter 5: Mastering Operations: Scheduling, Logistics, and Client Experience

The wheels of your mobile notary business are now turning. You've secured your commission, established your legal and financial foundations, and meticulously equipped your mobile office with all the essential tools. Now, it's time to talk about the very **heartbeat of your mobile business**: the day-to-day mastery of scheduling, seamless logistics, and delivering an exceptional client experience. This is where the rubber meets the road, where your meticulous planning translates directly into punctual arrivals, smooth signings, and, most importantly, satisfied customers who become your best advocates and the engine of your referral network. As I've learned through countless appointments with Mobile Notary by Derrick Spruill, operational excellence in these areas is what truly sets you apart from the competition and drives sustained profitability.

I. Introduction: The Heartbeat of Your Mobile Business

For a mobile notary, every single appointment isn't just a task; it's a meticulously choreographed mini-project. Each interaction involves a sequence of critical steps: initial planning and client communication, efficient travel, precise on-site execution of the notarial act, and diligent post-appointment follow-up. My approach to seamless service delivery has always been deeply rooted in the understanding that efficiency isn't merely about saving time or cutting corners; it's fundamentally about building an unshakeable reputation for reliability, professionalism, and trustworthiness. When you manage your operations flawlessly, you not only minimize stress for yourself but, more importantly, you dramatically reduce stress for your clients, who often come to you during critical, time-sensitive, or even emotionally charged moments in their lives. This commitment to operational excellence transforms a simple service into a memorable, positive experience.

Why Operational Efficiency Drives Profitability and Reputation: Operational efficiency is not just a desirable trait; it is the indispensable engine of your mobile notary business. Its impact is direct and profound across multiple facets of your enterprise:

- **Profitability:** Every minute saved in unproductive travel (e.g., avoiding traffic jams, taking optimized routes), every moment not spent waiting unnecessarily due to poor planning, or every administrative task streamlined, is a minute you can dedicate to another billable notarization or other income-generating activities. Efficient operations directly reduce your overhead costs, such as fuel consumption, vehicle wear and tear, and administrative labor. More importantly, these efficiencies directly maximize the number of billable notarizations you can realistically complete in a given day, thereby significantly boosting your overall revenue and, ultimately, your net profitability. It's the difference between merely being busy and being truly productive and financially successful.

- **Reputation:** Consistently arriving on time (or even a few minutes early), being impeccably prepared for every scenario, and executing signings smoothly and confidently builds a stellar, unshakeable reputation for reliability, professionalism, and meticulousness. This reputation is an invaluable intangible asset, leading directly to glowing Google reviews, enthusiastic word-of-mouth referrals, and a steady stream of repeat business. Clients remember the ease and peace of mind you provided. Conversely, consistent lateness, disorganization, or a rushed demeanor can quickly erode trust and severely damage your professional standing, leading to negative feedback and a reluctance for clients or referral sources to use your services again.
- **Client Satisfaction:** A seamless, well-organized, and stress-free experience for the client, from their very first inquiry to the final completion of the notarization, leaves a profoundly positive and lasting impression. This exceptional client experience is absolutely crucial for cultivating deep client loyalty, encouraging repeat business, and generating enthusiastic referrals, which, as we discussed in Chapter 25 of *Notary Knowledge: Reference Guide & Notary Bible*, are the lifeblood of a sustainable mobile notary business. When clients feel respected, informed, and efficiently served, they become powerful advocates for your brand, willingly sharing their positive experiences with others.
- **Work-Life Balance:** The demands of a mobile business can be taxing. However, when your operations are meticulously planned and executed with high efficiency, you significantly reduce personal stress and anxiety. Knowing your route, having sufficient buffer time between appointments, and proactively anticipating potential challenges allows you to focus calmly and entirely on the notarial act itself, rather than constantly worrying about traffic delays, being late for the next appointment, or managing unforeseen issues. This proactive approach contributes significantly to a healthier, more sustainable work-life balance, prevents professional burnout, and allows you to maintain a calm, composed, and positive demeanor during all client interactions.

My Approach to Seamless Service Delivery: My philosophy for achieving seamless service delivery is simple yet powerful: **anticipate, prepare, and communicate.** I strive to make every notary appointment feel effortless and stress-free for the client, even if there's complex choreography and meticulous behind-the-scenes management on my part. This involves a strategic blend of leveraging cutting-edge technology, adhering to strict operational protocols, and always prioritizing the client's experience above all else. It's about delivering a consistent, high-quality service that clients can rely on, every single time.

II. Scheduling Tools and Strategies: Optimizing Your Time

Effective scheduling is the absolutely first and most fundamental step in mastering your mobile operations. It's about intelligently organizing your day, week, and month to maximize your billable hours while simultaneously ensuring unwavering punctuality and supreme client satisfaction. This strategic approach transforms a chaotic workday into a streamlined, profitable endeavor.

Robust Calendar Management Systems (Your Digital Command Center): Your digital calendar is the central nervous system and the digital command center of your mobile notary business. It's where all your appointments, administrative tasks, and critical travel plans converge, providing a real-time overview of your availability and commitments.

- **Digital Calendars (Essential and Integrated):** I rely heavily on powerful digital calendars such as Google Calendar, Outlook Calendar, or Apple Calendar. These platforms are indispensable for managing my dynamic and often unpredictable schedule. They allow me to:
    - **Easily Add, Edit, and View Appointments:** I can quickly schedule new jobs, modify existing ones (e.g., if a client needs to reschedule), and view my entire day, week, or month at a glance from any device

(smartphone, tablet, laptop). This real-time accessibility is crucial for on-the-go management.

- **Set Automatic Reminders:** I create automatic reminders for myself (e.g., "Leave for next appointment in 15 mins," "Print loan package for 3 PM signing," "Follow up with client X") and, if integrated, for clients (e.g., "Your notary appointment is tomorrow at 2 PM. Please have your ID ready."). This significantly reduces the chance of missed appointments, ensures I am always prepared, and helps clients arrive ready for the signing.
- **Crucially, Block Out Realistic Travel Time:** This is a common and critical oversight for new notaries that can lead to significant overbooking, chronic lateness, and immense stress. I always meticulously block out realistic, dedicated travel time between appointments. This proactive measure prevents me from scheduling back-to-back appointments that are physically impossible to make, ensures I have adequate time to get from one location to the next, and significantly improves my punctuality. I often add extra buffer for unpredictable traffic in Northern Virginia, recognizing that traffic can be a major variable.
- **Color-Coding for Advanced Organization:** I use different colors for various types of appointments (e.g., green for high-value loan signings, blue for general notary work, red for personal time or administrative blocks, yellow for travel blocks, purple for apostille runs). This provides quick visual organization and clarity at a glance, allowing me to instantly understand my day's priorities, demands, and profitability at a glance.
- **Seamless Sync Across Devices:** I ensure my calendar seamlessly syncs across all my devices (smartphone, tablet, laptop) in real-time. This guarantees I always have access to my most current schedule, whether I'm in my car, at a client's location, or at my home office,

preventing scheduling conflicts and ensuring I'm always working with the most up-to-date information.

- **Online Booking Systems (Automation and Client Empowerment):** I highly recommend investing in a reputable online booking software (e.g., Calendly, Acuity Scheduling, Square Appointments, or specialized notary booking platforms like Snapdocs or NotaryDash for signing agents). These systems are invaluable for automating your scheduling process, enhancing client convenience, and significantly reducing your administrative burden, freeing up your time for billable work.
    - **Client Self-Service and Empowerment:** These systems empower clients to view my real-time availability and book appointments directly through an intuitive online interface, eliminating tedious and time-consuming back-and-forth communication via phone or email ("Are you free at 3 PM? How about 4:30?"). As I noted in *Quick & Easy Solutions: How to Increase Mobile Notary Business for More Success & Profit*, "Our clients can book appointments online through our website. These appointments are automatically fed into our calendars." This convenience is a major differentiator.
    - **Automated Confirmations and Reminders:** The systems automatically send professional confirmation emails/texts upon booking and timely reminders closer to the appointment time. This drastically reduces no-shows, ensures clients are fully prepared with their ID and documents, and minimizes the need for manual follow-ups.
    - **Integrated Intake Forms:** I integrate customizable intake forms that collect all necessary client information upfront (e.g., client name, precise address, document type, number of signers, specific notarization requests, special instructions) *before* the appointment is even confirmed. This saves significant time on initial phone calls and ensures I arrive fully prepared for the specific needs of the signing. As I

shared in *Quick & Easy Solutions*, "Our online data collection form easily captures the customer's name, address, service request, time, and payment."

- **Payment Integration (Optional Convenience):** Many systems allow for optional upfront payment or deposit collection, which can reduce payment friction at the time of service, minimize the risk of no-shows or last-minute cancellations, and improve your business's cash flow.

- **Automated Buffer Time Management:** I configure the system to automatically add buffer time between appointments, preventing accidental double-bookings and ensuring I have adequate transition time for travel, brief administrative tasks, and preparation for the next signing.
- **Service-Specific Booking Menus:** I allow clients to select the specific service they need from a detailed menu (e.g., "General Notary," "Loan Signing," "Apostille Facilitation," "I-9 Verification"). This ensures they book the correct type of appointment, which may have different time allocations, pricing, and required preparation.

Smart Scheduling Strategies (Optimizing Your Workday for Profitability and Efficiency): Beyond merely using technological tools, strategic thinking about your schedule is absolutely critical for maximizing efficiency, enhancing profitability, and significantly reducing operational stress. This is where your business acumen truly comes into play.

- **Batch Appointments Geographically (The "Route Optimization" Principle):** Whenever humanly possible, I actively try to schedule multiple appointments in the same geographical area or along a logical, efficient travel route. This "batching" strategy is a cornerstone of mobile notary profitability. It minimizes unproductive travel time, significantly reduces fuel costs, and directly maximizes the number of billable notarizations I can complete in a given day. For example, I might dedicate "North Side Tuesdays" or "South Side Thursdays" to cluster appointments in those respective areas, making one efficient loop rather than crisscrossing my service area multiple times a day. This is far more efficient than haphazardly scheduling.
- **Build in Generous Buffer Time (Anticipating the Unexpected):** I always build in realistic and generous buffer time between appointments (e.g., 15-30 minutes for simple acts, or 30-60 minutes or more for complex loan signings). This crucial buffer accounts for a myriad of unexpected delays like:
    - Heavy traffic or unexpected road closures (common in Northern Virginia).
    - Difficult or time-consuming parking challenges at a busy location.
    - Longer-than-expected signings (due to client questions, missing documents, or unforeseen complexities).
    - Brief client questions or administrative wrap-up tasks after an appointment. Rushing between appointments not only increases your personal stress and the likelihood of making errors (leading to potential liability, as discussed in *Notary Fraud Shield*), but it

can also severely diminish client satisfaction. A relaxed, unhurried notary is a better, more professional notary.

- **Define and Clearly Communicate Your Service Area and Travel Fee Tiers:** I clearly define my primary service area (e.g., "serving Loudoun and Fairfax Counties" or "within a 20-mile radius of downtown Herndon, VA"). I am transparent about my travel fees for appointments located outside this primary zone (as discussed in Chapter 4 of *The Mobile Notary Blueprint*). This manages client expectations upfront, prevents disputes, and ensures that longer trips are adequately compensated for profitability, rather than eroding your margins.
- **Set Clear and Manageable Availability (Preventing Burnout):** I communicate my working hours clearly on my website, GMB profile, and booking system. While flexibility and extended hours are key benefits of being a mobile notary, I avoid being "on call" 24/7, which can quickly lead to burnout, exhaustion, and diminished service quality. I define my boundaries for after-hours or weekend work and charge appropriate premium fees for these times to compensate for the personal sacrifice and increased demand. This protects your personal time and energy.
- **Prioritize High-Value Appointments (Strategic Revenue Management):** If I offer specialized services (e.g., Loan Signing Agent, Apostille Facilitation), I strategically prioritize scheduling those higher-paying assignments when my prime time slots are available. This maximizes my revenue per hour and ensures I am focusing my efforts on the most profitable aspects of my business, allowing for strategic growth.
- **Consider Dedicated "Office Days" or "Admin Blocks":** I dedicate specific days or blocks of time each week for administrative tasks, marketing efforts, continuing education, document scanning, or working on non-mobile notary services (like apostille processing or document printing). This prevents administrative tasks from encroaching on my mobile earning potential and ensures these vital business functions are not neglected, contributing to overall operational excellence.

III. Route Planning and On-Site Logistics: Precision in Motion

Efficient route planning ensures you get to your appointments punctually and safely, while meticulous on-site logistics ensure a smooth, professional, and compliant notarization experience, reflecting positively on your brand and fostering client trust.

Intelligent Route Planning and Navigation (Your Co-Pilot):

- **Reliable GPS Navigation Apps (Your Co-Pilot):** I always utilize current and highly reliable GPS navigation apps (e.g., Google Maps, Waze, Apple Maps) on my smartphone or a dedicated GPS device. These apps are indispensable for mobile notaries as they provide:
    - Real-time traffic updates, allowing you to dynamically adjust your route to avoid congestion and unexpected delays.
    - Suggestions for optimal routes based on current conditions, minimizing travel time and fuel consumption.
    - Accurate estimated arrival times (ETAs) that you can communicate directly to clients, managing their expectations effectively.
    - Multi-stop routing features, which are invaluable for batching appointments efficiently and creating a logical flow for your workday.
- **Proactive Traffic Checks and Contingency Planning:** I always check real-time traffic conditions *before* departing for *any* appointment, especially during peak rush hour times in Northern Virginia, where traffic can be notoriously heavy. I adjust my departure time accordingly or explore alternative routes if significant delays are predicted. Having a mental (or physical) contingency plan for unexpected traffic, sudden road closures, or vehicle issues can save immense stress and ensure punctuality.

- **Pre-Plan Parking Options:** For urban areas, commercial buildings, large apartment complexes, or medical facilities, I meticulously research parking options in advance. I look for available street parking, designated parking garages, or specific visitor spots. This proactive step avoids last-minute stress, prevents delays (and the need for clients to wait), and helps avoid potential parking violations or fines. Knowing where to park efficiently is a key time-saver and a mark of professionalism.
- **Familiarize Yourself with the Area (Beyond Just the Address):** If traveling to an unfamiliar neighborhood, a sprawling corporate campus, or a large residential complex, I briefly review the map or satellite view beforehand. I look for main entrances, specific building numbers, floor levels, and potential challenges (e.g., security gates, complex layouts). This brief reconnaissance can save significant time on arrival, prevent getting lost, and enhance your confidence when meeting the client.

On-Site Logistics for a Seamless Experience: Once you arrive at the client's location, your on-site actions directly influence the client's perception of your professionalism and your ability to perform a compliant notarization. Every detail contributes to the overall experience.

- **Punctual Arrival with a Composed Demeanor:** I aim to arrive 5-10 minutes early for appointments. This allows for parking, finding the exact location, and a brief moment to compose myself, gather my thoughts, and ensure all my supplies are readily accessible. I greet the client warmly and professionally, projecting a calm, confident, and reassuring presence. If I anticipate being late, I immediately communicate this to the client with an updated ETA, demonstrating respect for their time.
- **Professional Presentation and Organized Setup:** I always arrive neatly dressed in business casual or professional attire. I ensure all my notary supplies are organized and easily accessible in a professional bag. Your appearance, organized supplies, and efficient setup convey competence, respect, and reliability, building immediate trust with the client.
- **Request a Suitable Environment (Well-Lit, Quiet, Private):** Upon arrival, I politely but firmly request a well-lit, quiet, and private area for the notarization. This is absolutely crucial for multiple reasons:
    - **Proper ID Verification:** You need good, consistent lighting to meticulously scrutinize security features on identification documents and accurately compare the photo to the signer's face.
    - **Assessing Signer Awareness and Willingness:** A quiet, private environment minimizes distractions and

allows you to accurately assess the signer's demeanor, alertness, and understanding, free from undue influence or coercion from third parties (as discussed in *Notary Fraud Shield*).

- **Maintaining Privacy and Confidentiality:** It protects the client's sensitive document contents and personal information from being overheard or seen by unauthorized individuals.
- **Ensuring a Clear Seal Impression:** Good lighting and a stable, flat surface are essential for applying a clear, legible notary seal impression without smudges or errors.

- **Secure Signing Surface:** I ensure there's a suitable, flat, and stable surface (ideally a table or desk) for the signer to comfortably sign documents and for me to apply my seal. I strictly avoid attempting notarizations on laps, uneven surfaces, or in moving vehicles, as this compromises document integrity, seal clarity, and your ability to perform the act correctly and compliantly.
- **Maintain Control of Documents and Supplies:** Throughout the entire appointment, I always maintain physical control of the documents being notarized, my notary journal, and my notary seal. I never leave them unattended, out of my sight, or allow unauthorized individuals to handle them. This is a critical security measure to prevent tampering, theft, or unauthorized use of your official tools, directly protecting you from liability (as emphasized in *Notary Fraud Shield*).
- **Post-Notarization Wrap-Up and Final Check:** After the notarization is complete and before I depart, I take a moment to meticulously review the entire signed package one last time. I check for:
    - All required signatures, initials, and dates are present in the correct locations.
    - All notarial certificates are correctly completed with my signature and seal, without blanks or errors.
    - No blank spaces within the documents that should have been filled in.

- Documents are in the correct order for return (e.g., originals vs. copies, specific stacking order for loan packages).
- My journal entry is complete and accurate. This final quality control step is absolutely crucial for catching and correcting any last-minute errors before they become costly problems, saving you and your client immense frustration and potential financial repercussions. I always thank the client for their business.

A True Story: The Hospital Visit and the Power of Presence

I recall a particularly memorable call that truly underscored the importance of meticulous scheduling, on-site logistics, and maintaining composure under pressure. It was a rainy night, and I received a phone call from a woman asking for a notary. We made an appointment to meet at a local hospital. As I prepared to travel, I received a second, urgent phone call from a doctor at the exact location, telling me to hurry because the client was undergoing emergency surgery. I adjusted my route and arrived earlier than expected after a short, foggy drive.

Once I arrived at the hospital, the environment was a whirlwind of activity. The commotion in the hallways and the client's room was palpable. My client was experiencing significant pain from a recent car accident, yet he was remarkably able to talk and even make jokes, displaying incredible resilience. His girlfriend and assistant were with him. It was 2:00 a.m., and he desperately needed papers notarized to release his vehicle from the impound, a critical step before his surgery.

In that chaotic, urgent, and emotionally charged environment, maintaining my composure and adhering to my on-site protocols was paramount. I politely but firmly requested a quiet corner of the room, ensuring enough light to verify his ID and a stable surface for him to sign. Despite the surrounding activity and the urgency, I focused solely on him, verifying his identity carefully, assessing his willingness and awareness through direct conversation, and ensuring every signature was correctly placed and every notarial act flawlessly executed.

He said something to me that night, in the midst of his pain and the hospital's bustle, that I will never forget: "Never drive when in rage; driving requires too much focus. Don't get caught up in a conversation over the phone and forget where you are. Let everyone know—to stay in the moment." This powerful message, delivered by someone in immense pain, profoundly reinforced my commitment to being **fully present and focused** during every signing, regardless of external pressures or distractions. My meticulous scheduling and built-in buffer time (as discussed earlier in this chapter) allowed me the crucial space to respond to this emergency without rushing, ensuring I could give him my undivided attention and perform my duties with the precision he deserved. It was a powerful testament to how operational excellence allows us to be truly human, empathetic, and helpful in critical moments, transforming a stressful situation into a smoothly handled transaction.

IV. Communication with Clients: The Cornerstone of Professionalism and Trust

Clear, proactive, and professional communication with clients is paramount for managing expectations, building unwavering trust, and ensuring smooth, efficient, and satisfactory appointments. It defines the entire client experience, from their first thought of needing a notary to their final interaction and beyond.

Pre-Appointment Communication (Setting Clear Expectations and Ensuring Preparedness):

- **Confirm Appointments Religiously:** I always confirm appointments (via text, email, or phone call) the day before or the morning of the appointment. This dramatically reduces no-shows, minimizes wasted travel time, and ensures the client is fully prepared for your arrival, leading to a more efficient signing.

- **Provide Clear, Actionable Instructions:** I meticulously remind clients of what they need to have ready *before* my arrival. I am specific, concise, and provide actionable bullet points to ensure they are fully prepared:
    - "Please have your valid, unexpired, government-issued photo ID (like a driver's license or U.S. passport) ready for each signer." I often specify that photos of IDs are not acceptable for traditional notarization.
    - "Ensure your document is completely filled out but unsigned (for Jurats) or signed but ready for acknowledgment (for Acknowledgments)." This prevents delays on-site.
    - "Confirm all signers who need notarization will be physically present." This avoids wasted trips.
    - "If your document requires additional disinterested witnesses, please have them present and identified, as I cannot act as a document witness." This proactive guidance prevents delays and frustration on-site, ensuring the signing can proceed as planned.
- **Communicate Fees Transparently and Upfront:** I reiterate my notary fees and travel fees upfront, as discussed in Chapter 4 of *The Mobile Notary Blueprint*. I provide a clear, itemized quote to avoid any surprises or disputes at the time of service. Transparency builds trust and prevents negative reviews.
- **Estimated Time of Arrival (ETA):** I provide a realistic ETA when I am en route to the appointment. If unforeseen circumstances (e.g., heavy traffic, a prior signing running longer than expected) cause me to be early or late, I immediately communicate the updated ETA to the client via text or call. This proactive communication manages expectations, demonstrates respect for their time, and allows them to adjust their schedule accordingly.

During the Appointment Communication (Guiding with Clarity and Professionalism):

- **Explain Your Role and Boundaries:** I briefly and clearly explain my role as an impartial witness and what I *can* and *cannot* do (e.g., "I am a Notary Public, not an attorney, so I cannot give legal advice or explain the document's content"). This manages expectations, prevents the Unauthorized Practice of Law (UPL), and sets clear boundaries for the interaction.
- **Walk Through the Process:** I briefly explain the steps I will take during the notarization (e.g., "First, I'll verify your ID and complete my journal entry, then we'll proceed with the signing and notarization of your document"). This helps the client feel informed, comfortable, and understand the flow of the process.
- **Address Questions Professionally:** I answer any questions within the strict scope of my duties professionally and patiently. If a question falls outside my scope (e.g., legal advice), I politely but firmly refer them to the appropriate professional (e.g., "For questions about the legal implications of this document, you'll need to consult with an attorney."). This reinforces your professionalism and legal compliance.

Post-Appointment Communication (Reinforcing Satisfaction and Encouraging Referrals):

- **Provide Detailed Receipt:** I always provide a professional, itemized receipt for services rendered, detailing all charges. This is good business practice, promotes transparency, and provides the client with a clear record for their own accounting or reimbursement.
- **Shipping Confirmation (for LSAs):** If I am responsible for shipping documents (common for Loan Signing Agents), I provide the tracking number promptly after dropping off the package at the courier service. This proactive update is highly valued by clients and title companies, providing peace of mind.

- **Follow-Up Email/Text (Optional but Highly Recommended):** A polite, brief message thanking them for their business and offering future assistance can significantly enhance client satisfaction and encourage positive reviews. This shows you care beyond the immediate transaction and fosters loyalty.
- **Request for Reviews:** I politely ask satisfied clients to leave a review on my Google My Business profile or other relevant platforms (e.g., NNA Notary Locator, Yelp). I make it easy for them by providing a direct link. Positive reviews are your most powerful marketing tool, acting as social proof that drives new business.

V. Safety and Professional Conduct on the Road: Protecting Yourself and Your Brand

As a mobile notary, your personal safety is paramount. You are often traveling to unfamiliar locations and meeting new people, sometimes during non-traditional hours. Integrating robust safety protocols into your logistics is non-negotiable and a critical aspect of your operational excellence. Your conduct on the road directly reflects on your professional brand.

Personal Safety Measures:

- **Inform a Trusted Contact of Your Schedule:** This is a critical safety protocol that I adhere to diligently. I always let a trusted friend, family member, or colleague know my detailed schedule for the day, including client addresses, contact numbers, and estimated times of arrival and departure for each appointment. I establish a check-in protocol (e.g., a quick text after each appointment is completed). This provides a crucial safety net and accountability, especially when working during non-traditional hours or in unfamiliar areas.
- **Share Location (Optional, but Recommended):** For certain appointments, especially those in unfamiliar, isolated, or potentially high-risk areas, I consider using a smartphone's

real-time location-sharing feature (e.g., via Google Maps, Find My Friends) with a trusted contact. This allows someone to monitor your progress and know your whereabouts, providing an added layer of security and peace of mind.

- **Trust Your Gut (and Prioritize Safety Above All Else):** Your intuition is a powerful safety tool. If a situation, location, or client interaction feels unsafe, uncomfortable, suspicious, or simply "off" at any point, trust that feeling. Do not hesitate. Politely excuse yourself and leave the premises immediately. Your personal safety is paramount and should *never* be compromised for a notarization fee. Document any such incidents in your notary journal (date, time, location, reason for refusal) and consider reporting them to local law enforcement or your commissioning authority. This is a non-negotiable aspect of your "Power of Refusal" (as detailed in *Notary Fraud Shield*).
- **Public Meeting Places (Strategic Choice):** For initial meetings with new or unknown clients, especially for general notary work, I often consider suggesting a public meeting place (e.g., a well-lit coffee shop, a public library, a co-working space lobby, or a business center) if appropriate for the document type and client's comfort. This adds a layer of safety and transparency, as there are usually other people around.
- **Self-Defense Item (Optional, with Caution and Training):** If I feel it's necessary for personal safety, I research and comply with all local and state laws regarding permissible self-defense items (e.g., pepper spray, personal alarm, Taser). If you choose to carry one, ensure you receive proper training on its safe, legal, and responsible use. Always prioritize de-escalation and avoidance strategies over confrontation.
- **First-Aid Kit:** A small, basic first-aid kit for minor cuts, scrapes, or other small emergencies (e.g., bandages, antiseptic wipes, pain relievers) can be invaluable to have readily accessible in your vehicle for unexpected situations.

Professional Conduct on the Road: Your conduct, even when not directly performing a notarization, reflects on your professional brand and reputation.

- **Maintain Professional Attire:** I consistently dress in business casual or professional attire. Your appearance directly impacts your client's perception of your professionalism and trustworthiness. Clients are more likely to trust a well-dressed notary. I keep a spare, clean, wrinkle-free outfit in my car for emergencies or unexpected spills, ensuring I always look presentable, even after a long day of driving.
- **Vehicle Maintenance and Cleanliness:** I keep my vehicle clean, well-maintained, and adequately fueled for reliability. A clean, presentable vehicle reflects professionalism and ensures you arrive reliably and safely at every appointment, preventing breakdowns and delays that could impact your schedule. Regular vehicle maintenance is a critical operational cost to factor into your business plan.
- **Confidentiality in Transit:** I always maintain strict client confidentiality, especially when traveling between appointments or in public spaces. Ensure documents containing sensitive Personally Identifiable Information (PII) are secured in your notary bag and not visible to unauthorized eyes. Avoid leaving documents on seats where they could be seen or stolen. This is a crucial aspect of your ethical duty of confidentiality.
- **Ethical Driving:** I drive safely and courteously. Avoid speeding, aggressive driving, or distracted driving, as this reflects poorly on your professional image, increases accident risk, and can lead to unnecessary stress and delays. Your conduct on the road is an extension of your professionalism.

Conclusion

Efficient scheduling and meticulous logistics are the unsung heroes and the foundational pillars of a successful, profitable, and professional mobile notary business. By strategically utilizing digital tools for calendar management and online booking, optimizing travel routes through intelligent planning, building in ample buffer time to absorb unforeseen delays, and maintaining clear, proactive, and professional communication with clients, notaries can maximize their profitability, ensure unwavering punctuality, and consistently deliver an exceptional customer experience. Coupled with an unwavering focus on personal safety and impeccable professional conduct, mastery of scheduling and logistics empowers mobile notaries to operate with confidence, efficiency, and excellence in every appointment, solidifying their reputation as reliable, indispensable, and highly sought-after service providers in today's dynamic marketplace. Your preparedness is not just a convenience; it is your competitive edge and a cornerstone of your professional integrity.

Chapter 6: Marketing and Growth: Attracting and Retaining Your Client Base

Welcome to the final chapter of **"The Mobile Notary Blueprint: Launching and Managing Your On-Demand Business."** We've

covered the compelling reasons to go mobile (Chapter 1), meticulously built your legal and financial foundations (Chapter 2), equipped your mobile office for on-the-go excellence (Chapter 3), and mastered the art of strategic pricing (Chapter 4) and efficient operations (Chapter 5). Now, it's time to bring it all together by focusing on the very lifeblood of any thriving enterprise: **marketing and growth**. As I've learned through building Mobile Notary by Derrick Spruill and expanding my "Notary Knowledge by Derrick Spruill" podcast, simply being a great notary isn't enough; you need to effectively attract and retain clients to ensure sustainable success. This chapter will provide comprehensive strategies for building a strong brand, attracting a steady stream of new clients, fostering unwavering loyalty, and ensuring the long-term growth and resilience of your mobile notary business.

I. Introduction: Beyond the Notarization – Building a Brand

When I first started Mobile Notary by Derrick Spruill, I had no intention of just passing out flyers or going from location to location seeking customers at the wrong time. I knew instinctively that the immense power of the internet could help customers find me precisely when they needed a service, wherever they were. My goal wasn't just to be a notary who performed acts; it was to build a reputable, trustworthy brand that stood out in a crowded marketplace. As I wrote in *Quick & Easy Solutions: How to Increase Mobile Notary Business for More Success & Profit*, "I need to build a level of trust for a customer to trust that I will not make a mistake with their documents, and they can verify whom I say I am. Funny, affirming the notary, but true. I need to prove who I am first." This realization was pivotal: my brand, my online presence, and my reputation would be my primary marketing tools.

Why Marketing is Essential for Sustainable Growth: Marketing is not an optional add-on; it's the indispensable engine that drives sustainable growth for your mobile notary business. It directly impacts:

- **Visibility:** Ensuring potential clients can actually *find* you when they are actively searching for notary services. Without effective marketing, even the best notary remains invisible.
- **Credibility:** Building trust and professionalism *before* you even meet a client. A strong brand presence signals reliability and expertise, which is crucial for a public official.
- **Client Acquisition:** Attracting new business consistently, moving beyond sporadic, one-off jobs to a steady stream of new opportunities.
- **Retention & Referrals:** Fostering loyalty that leads to invaluable repeat business and enthusiastic word-of-mouth referrals, which are the most powerful form of marketing.
- **Competitive Advantage:** Differentiating yourself in a crowded market, allowing you to stand out from competitors and justify your pricing.

My Philosophy on Client Acquisition and Retention: My philosophy is centered on transparency, unwavering professionalism, and consistent value. I believe that by making it incredibly easy for clients to find me, clearly understand my services and pricing, and experience top-tier professionalism from the first contact to the final handshake, they will not only become repeat customers but also enthusiastic advocates for my business. This belief is why I've personally invested hundreds of hours into meticulously building and optimizing my online presence and relentlessly focusing on exceptional customer service. I aim to create a seamless, positive experience that clients will remember and recommend.

II. Building a Professional Online Presence: Your Digital Storefront

In today's digital-first world, your online presence is your 24/7 storefront, constantly working to attract and inform clients. It's often the first, and sometimes only, point of contact for potential clients. A meticulously crafted and strategically managed online footprint is absolutely essential for discoverability, credibility, and establishing your brand authority.

Professional Website (Your 24/7 Information Hub):

- **Purpose:** Your website is the cornerstone of your entire online presence, acting as your 24/7 digital storefront and primary information hub. It's where clients go for detailed information about your services, your qualifications, and to make booking decisions.
- **Key Elements:**
    - **Mobile-Friendly and Responsive Design:** This is absolutely non-negotiable. The vast majority of local searches for services are performed on mobile devices. Your website *must* load quickly (within 2-3 seconds) and display correctly and intuitively on all smartphones and tablets, ensuring a seamless user experience. A slow or non-responsive site will deter potential clients and negatively impact your search engine ranking.

- **Clear Value Proposition:** Immediately communicate what you do, who you serve, and your unique benefits (e.g., "Convenient Mobile Notary Services in Northern Virginia," "Expert Loan Signing Agent for Your Region"). This instantly tells visitors if you meet their needs.
- **Comprehensive Service List:** Detail *all* your offerings (general notary work, loan signings, apostille services, I-9 verification, RON, etc.). Use clear, concise, and benefit-oriented language for each service.
- **Defined Service Area:** Clearly state the geographical areas you serve (e.g., Loudoun, Fairfax, Prince William Counties in Northern Virginia). This helps local clients find you and manages expectations regarding travel.
- **Transparent Pricing:** Explain your pricing philosophy and structure (referencing Chapter 4 of *The Mobile Notary Blueprint*). As I learned from *Quick & Easy Solutions*, "We set our prices online. Every service has a fixed price... This will provide confidence for each of your clients and possibly repeat business." Clarity around fees builds trust.
- **Prominent Contact Information:** Display your phone number (clickable on mobile), professional email, and a user-friendly contact form prominently on every page of your website, especially in the header and footer. Make it effortless for clients to reach you.
- **Testimonials/Reviews Section:** Dedicate a prominent section to showcase positive client feedback and testimonials. This is powerful social proof that builds confidence in potential clients.
- **Blog/Resources:** A blog with helpful articles on notary tips (e.g., "What ID to bring for notarization," "How to prepare for a loan signing") establishes you as an expert and boosts your Search Engine Optimization (SEO) by providing fresh, relevant content.

- **My Experience:** I personally invested a significant amount of time building the Mobile Notary by Derrick Spruill website with SEO meticulously in mind. As I shared in *Quick & Easy Solutions*, "The website could be better, but it compares well to large familiar household name brand companies and others when we use the Lighthouse plug-in to measure the speed and performance of the websites." This dedication to performance and user experience is crucial for organic search visibility.

Google My Business (GMB) Profile (Local Search Dominance):

- **Purpose:** For local service businesses like mobile notaries, your Google My Business (GMB) profile is arguably the single most important online asset. It directly controls your appearance in Google Maps, the local "3-pack" search results (the top three local businesses shown for a search), and general local search queries.
- **Optimization:**
    - **Claim and Verify:** This is the absolute first and crucial step to control your listing.
    - **Accurate & Consistent NAP:** Ensure your Name, Address (if home-based, use a service area business profile that hides your street address but defines your service radius), and Phone number are identical and consistent across *all* your online listings. This NAP (Name, Address, Phone) consistency is vital for local SEO and helps Google trust your business information.
    - **Complete Profile:** Fill out every single section of your GMB profile: business hours, detailed services list, high-quality photos (of yourself, your supplies, your vehicle), and regular posts (sharing updates, promotions, or helpful tips). As I noted in *Quick & Easy Solutions*, "Adding all this information builds creditability for your website connection on the Internet. It may not happen all in one sitting, so continue to add new information over time. Internet crawlers love to find new information."

- **Actively Manage Reviews:** Encourage satisfied clients to leave Google reviews. The volume and quality of your Google reviews are massive trust signals for potential clients and significantly impact your local search ranking. Respond professionally to *all* reviews, both positive and negative, in a timely manner. As I shared in *Quick & Easy Solutions*, asking customers for reviews "has helped us to skyrocket to the top of the webpage search as credibility from Google. Google looks to us as an authority figure when it comes to mobile notary services in the areas we serve." This took time, but the payoff was immense.

Online Directories and Notary-Specific Platforms:

- **Purpose:** Listing your business on relevant online directories and specialized notary platforms significantly increases your visibility beyond just Google Search, and helps build crucial trust signals across the web.
- **Key Platforms:**

  - **National Notary Association (NNA) Notary Locator:** If you're an NNA member, ensure your profile on their Notary Locator is complete, detailed, and optimized. This is a primary and highly trusted source for clients and businesses specifically seeking qualified notaries.
  - **Signing Agent Websites/Platforms:** If you're a Loan Signing Agent (LSA), create comprehensive profiles

on platforms frequently used by title companies and signing services to assign closings (e.g., Snapdocs, NotaryDash, SigningOrder.com, SigningAgent.com). These platforms are essential for securing loan signing work.

- **General Business Directories:** Ensure your business is listed on major general business directories like Yelp, Yellow Pages, and your local Chamber of Commerce directories. Again, verify that your Name, Address, Phone (NAP) information is absolutely consistent across all these listings.

Social Media (Strategic Professional Use):

- **Purpose:** Not all social media platforms are equally relevant or effective for a notary business. Focus your efforts strategically on platforms that align with professional networking and content sharing, always maintaining strict impartiality and professionalism.
- **Key Platforms:**
    - **LinkedIn:** This is an essential platform for professional networking. Use it to connect with real estate agents, loan officers, attorneys, title company professionals, HR managers, and other potential referral sources. Share industry insights, news related to notarization or real estate, and maintain a professional profile that highlights your specialized services and certifications.
    - **Facebook Business Page:** Can be useful for local community engagement. Share helpful tips for local residents (e.g., "Why you need a mobile notary for your will"), announce special availability, and run targeted local ads to reach potential clients in your service area. Encourage reviews on your Facebook page.
    - **Instagram (Optional, Visual Branding):** Can be used for visual branding, sharing professional photos of your setup (without compromising client privacy),

or showcasing your professional personality. While less direct for lead generation, it can build brand awareness and a more relatable image. Focus on clean, professional aesthetics.

- **Content Strategy:** Develop a consistent content strategy across your chosen platforms. Share helpful tips (e.g., "What ID to bring for notarization," "How to prepare for a loan signing," "The benefits of an Advance Healthcare Directive"), industry news, or positive client testimonials (with permission). **Crucially, always avoid personal opinions, political content, or anything that could compromise your impartiality or professional image as a public official.** Your content should be informative, helpful, and strictly professional. As I mentioned in *Quick & Easy Solutions*, "Use social media to promote your web presence... This is a great way to let the world know your business exists."

Professional Email Address and Communication:

- **Branded Email:** Always use a professional, branded email address (e.g., `yourname@yourbusinessname.com` or `info@yourbusinessname.com`) rather than a generic Gmail, Yahoo, or Hotmail address. This instantly enhances your credibility and professionalism in every communication, signaling that you are a legitimate business. As I noted in *Quick & Easy Solutions*, "It looks professional and easy to associate with the business name... It makes for great branding."
- **Email Signature:** Configure your email signature to automatically include your logo, business name, your full name, your professional title (Notary Public, Loan Signing Agent), your phone number, your website link, and perhaps a direct link for clients to book a notary or leave a review. This provides all necessary information and reinforces your brand with every email.

III. Networking Strategies: Cultivating Robust Referral Sources

While a strong online presence is vital for discoverability, proactive networking and building genuine, reciprocal relationships are the "gold standard" for consistent, high-quality client acquisition. Referral business is often the most lucrative and reliable source of new clients because it comes with an inherent level of trust already established by the referrer.

Identifying Target Referral Sources: Where Your Ideal Clients Are: Focus your networking efforts strategically on professionals and organizations who frequently require notarization services for their clients but typically do not perform them in-house, or who specifically need specialized mobile notary expertise. Think about who interacts with individuals needing notarized documents *before* they even consider a notary.

- **Title Companies and Escrow Officers:** (Highest priority for LSAs). These entities are the central hubs for real estate closings. They constantly need reliable, meticulously accurate LSAs to facilitate loan signings, often on tight deadlines. They value notaries who can ensure a flawless closing package.
- **Real Estate Agents:** Both buyer's and seller's agents frequently encounter clients needing notarizations for various transaction documents (e.g., purchase agreements, disclosures, affidavits, powers of attorney related to property). They are excellent sources for general notary work and can refer you directly to their clients for loan signings, especially if you establish yourself as an LSA.
- **Attorneys:** Lawyers across various specializations are constant sources of notarization needs:
    - **Estate Planning Attorneys:** Routinely need notarizations for wills, trusts, powers of attorney (POAs), and medical directives. They require notaries who understand the sensitivity and critical nature of

these documents, and who can assess signer awareness.
  - **Family Law Attorneys:** Often require notarizations for divorce decrees, child custody agreements, prenuptial agreements, and various affidavits.
  - **Business Attorneys:** Need notarizations for contracts, corporate resolutions, articles of incorporation, and other foundational business documents.
  - **Immigration Attorneys:** Frequently require notarizations for affidavits of support, sworn statements, and other immigration forms. They need notaries who are reliable and understand the urgency of immigration deadlines.
- **Hospitals, Nursing Homes, and Assisted Living Facilities:** These institutions often have patients or residents who need medical directives, powers of attorney, or other crucial documents notarized but cannot leave the facility. Build relationships with social workers, discharge planners, patient advocates, or administrative staff who coordinate these services. They need notaries who are compassionate, professional, and understand the nuances of assessing capacity.
- **Banks and Credit Unions:** While larger banks may have in-house notaries, many smaller branches or credit unions do not, or their notaries may not be available after hours or for mobile services. They can be excellent referral sources for clients needing mobile notarizations for various financial documents.
- **Mortgage Brokers and Loan Officers:** These professionals originate loans and have a direct need for reliable LSAs to ensure smooth and timely closings for their borrowers. They value notaries who can provide a seamless signing experience that reflects well on their own service.
- **Local Businesses (Small to Large):** Small businesses, accounting firms, human resources departments, and even large corporations may need regular notarizations for contracts, corporate documents, vendor agreements, or I-9 verifications for remote employees.

- **Auto Dealerships and DMV Service Providers:** Often need notarizations for vehicle title transfers, powers of attorney for vehicle registration, or bills of sale.
- **Jail/Correctional Facilities:** Notaries are frequently needed for inmates to sign legal documents (e.g., powers of attorney, affidavits, child custody papers). Establishing contact with facility administrators or legal services departments can open up a consistent niche.

Building Relationships: The Art of Connection: Effective networking is about building genuine, long-term relationships based on trust and mutual benefit, not just a transactional exchange of contact information.

- **Initial Professional Outreach:** Send a concise, professional introduction email or make a targeted phone call. Clearly explain your mobile notary services, highlight your unique value proposition (e.g., "I offer reliable, after-hours mobile notary services, which can help your clients complete signings quickly without disrupting their workday"), and explain how you can genuinely make *their* job easier or solve a pain point for their clients.
- **Offer In-Person Meetings:** If appropriate, offer to meet for a brief coffee or lunch to discuss their specific needs and how your services can seamlessly integrate into their workflow. This personal touch builds rapport far more effectively than email alone.
- **Provide Value First:** Don't just ask for business; offer value. Offer to provide free, brief notary-related information sessions for their staff (e.g., "Understanding Notary Basics for Real Estate Agents," "Common I-9 Errors to Avoid," "Navigating Advance Directives"). This positions you as a knowledgeable resource and builds trust.
- **Be Impeccably Responsive and Reliable:** When a referral source sends you business, your performance is a direct reflection on them. Be impeccably professional, punctual, accurate, and communicative. Provide prompt updates on signing completion. This builds deep trust and encourages

consistent repeat referrals. A single flawless transaction is worth dozens of cold calls.

- **Consistent Follow-Up and Relationship Nurturing:** Don't just send a thank-you note after a referral (though always do that!). Periodically check in with your referral sources via email, phone, or a brief visit to maintain the relationship. Share relevant industry news or updates. Remember personal details about their business or interests.
- **Reciprocal Referrals:** Actively look for opportunities to refer clients *back* to your professional partners. If you encounter clients who need services your referral sources provide (e.g., a client needing an estate planning attorney), refer them. This fosters a truly mutually beneficial relationship and demonstrates your commitment to their success.

Professional Organizations and Community Involvement: Expanding Your Sphere of Influence: Active participation in relevant groups significantly expands your network and builds your reputation.

- **Chamber of Commerce:** Join your local Chamber of Commerce. Attend networking events and business expos to meet other local business owners.
- **Industry Associations:** Join local chapters of real estate agent associations, bar associations (many have affiliate memberships), or mortgage broker associations. Attend their meetings.
- **Community Groups:** Get involved in local community groups or volunteer organizations. This builds your reputation and visibility within the community.
- **Online Professional Groups:** Participate in relevant LinkedIn groups or online forums, offering helpful insights and establishing yourself as a knowledgeable resource.

IV. Direct Client Acquisition Strategies: Reaching Your Audience

While referrals are the "gold standard," direct acquisition strategies are crucial for complementing networking efforts, filling your calendar, and providing immediate revenue streams. These strategies focus on directly reaching and converting individuals and businesses who are actively searching for notary services.

Optimizing Your Online Presence (Revisited for Direct Acquisition): As extensively discussed in Chapter 24 of *Notary Knowledge: Reference Guide & Notary Bible*, your online presence is your primary tool for direct client acquisition. It's where potential clients find you when they have an immediate need.

- **Hyper-Focused Local SEO:** Beyond general optimization, focus on hyper-local SEO tactics. Ensure your Google My Business profile is fully optimized with specific service categories, accurate service areas, and compelling photos. Actively solicit and respond to Google reviews, as these are paramount for local search ranking. Ensure your website is mobile-friendly and uses local keywords naturally in its content (e.g., "mobile notary specificneighborhood ," "loan signing agent zipcode"). Build local citations (mentions of your business name, address, phone) across various online directories.
- **Targeted Online Advertising:** Consider running targeted local online advertising campaigns.
    - **Google Ads (Search Campaigns):** Bid on keywords like "mobile notary near me," "notary public yourcity

      ," "loan signing agent yourcounty" These ads appear at the top of Google search results when clients are actively searching for your services.

    - **Facebook/Instagram Ads:** Target specific demographics (e.g., homeowners, small business owners, real estate professionals) within your service area with ads highlighting your convenience and specialized services. Set a clear budget and monitor your ad performance closely to optimize your spend.

Responding to Inquiries (Speed, Clarity, and Professionalism): Once a client finds you online, your response to their inquiry is the critical conversion point.

- **Rapid Response is Paramount:** In the mobile notary business, speed often wins the job. When a client calls or submits an online inquiry, respond as quickly as humanly possible, ideally within minutes, not hours. Clients often contact the first notary who responds.
- **Clear and Comprehensive Quoting:** Provide a clear, itemized quote for your services upfront. This quote should detail:
  - The state-regulated notary fee per signature/act.
  - Your travel fee (broken down by mileage tier or flat rate).
  - Any specialized service fees (e.g., loan signing fee, apostille facilitation fee, I-9 fee).
  - Any ancillary fees (e.g., printing, waiting fees).
  - The total estimated cost. This transparency builds trust and prevents misunderstandings.
- **Professional and Helpful Communication:** Maintain a polite, helpful, and professional tone in all communications (phone, email, text). Answer their questions clearly, confirm your availability, and reiterate what they need to have ready for the appointment (ID, unsigned document, all signers present). Be proactive in guiding them through the process.

Cold Outreach (Ethical and Strategic Considerations): While often challenging, targeted cold outreach can be effective for reaching specific types of businesses or professionals who might not be actively searching for a notary.

- **Highly Targeted Approach:** Do not just mass-email. Research specific law firms (e.g., estate planning, immigration), title companies, or HR departments that you believe have a consistent need for your services. Identify the specific person to contact (e.g., office manager, paralegal, HR director).
- **Focus on Value Proposition:** Your outreach message should immediately focus on how you can solve *their* problems or make *their* job easier. (e.g., "I offer reliable, after-hours, mobile loan signing services that can help your clients close quickly and conveniently," or "I provide on-site I-9 verification for your remote hires, ensuring federal compliance").
- **Compliance with Laws:** Always comply with telemarketing laws, unsolicited email regulations (CAN-SPAM Act), and any specific industry regulations (e.g., RESPA for real estate). Respect "do not call" lists.
- **Persistence with Professionalism:** Cold outreach often requires persistence. Follow up politely but don't be pushy.

Referral Programs and Incentives: Formalizing referral programs can incentivize both past clients and professional partners to send you more business.

- **Client Referral Program:** Offer a small discount on a future service or a modest incentive (e.g., a $10 gift card) to existing clients who refer new business to you that results in a completed notarization. This encourages word-of-mouth.
- **Professional Referral Program:** For your professional referral sources (e.g., real estate agents, attorneys), consider a formal or informal referral agreement. This might involve a small finder's fee (ensure it complies with all state laws and ethical guidelines, especially for real estate transactions, where RESPA regulations strictly prohibit kickbacks for referrals of settlement services). Alternatively, focus on reciprocal referrals and providing exceptional service as the primary incentive.

V. Providing Excellent Customer Service: Your Ultimate Marketing Tool

Excellent customer service is not merely a desirable trait; it is an indispensable, strategic imperative for the sustained growth and resounding success of a mobile notary business. It's your most powerful marketing tool, transforming satisfied clients into enthusiastic advocates.

The Indispensable Role of Excellent Customer Service:

- **Differentiation:** In a crowded market, exceptional customer service sets you apart.
- **Trust and Credibility:** A positive service experience builds immediate and profound trust.
- **Repeat Business:** Satisfied clients are highly likely to use your services again.
- **Generating Invaluable Referrals:** Delighted clients become your most effective marketing team, eagerly referring you.
- **Fueling Positive Online Reviews:** Excellent service directly translates into glowing online reviews, which are powerful social proof.
- **Effective Problem Resolution:** Strong customer service skills enable you to resolve issues amicably, preventing negative feedback.
- **Elevating Your Professional Reputation:** Consistently delivering excellent service builds a stellar reputation, opening doors to higher-value clients.
- **Enhancing Client Lifetime Value (CLV):** Fostering loyalty increases the total revenue generated from each client over time.

Pillars of Excellent Customer Service:

- **Responsiveness and Timely Communication:** Prompt replies, clear communication at every stage (inquiry, scheduling, en route, post-signing), and proactive expectation management.

- **Unwavering Professionalism in Every Interaction:** Impeccable appearance and demeanor, clear and respectful verbal/written communication, absolute respect for privacy and confidentiality, punctuality, and meticulous preparedness.
- **Unwavering Clarity and Transparency (Especially with Fees):** Upfront, itemized quoting, no hidden fees, and providing professional receipts.
- **Genuine Empathy and Patient Guidance:** Understanding client needs and stressors, practicing active listening, patience, protecting vulnerable signers with compassion, and cultural sensitivity.
- **Proactive Problem Resolution and Accountability:** Owning mistakes, rectifying errors promptly, de-escalating upset clients, and following through on commitments.

Customer Service at Every Touchpoint:

- **Initial Inquiry:** Speed, clarity, professionalism.
- **Scheduling and Pre-Appointment:** Clear confirmation, proactive reminders, ETA communication.
- **On-Site Appointment:** Punctual arrival, professional greeting, clear setup, efficient process, explaining notarial act clearly, final document review, expressing gratitude.
- **Post-Appointment Follow-Up:** Providing detailed receipts, shipping confirmation (for LSAs), optional follow-up emails/texts, and requests for reviews.

The Power of Reviews and Referrals: Your Ultimate Marketing Engine:

- **Encouraging Reviews Systematically:** Politely ask every satisfied client to leave a review on your Google My Business profile and other relevant platforms.
- **Responding to Reviews:** Always thank clients for positive feedback. For negative reviews, respond professionally, calmly, and offer to resolve the issue offline.

- **Cultivating Referrals:** Deliver excellence consistently, build reciprocal relationships with partners, and formally thank referral sources.

VI. Strategic Growth and Long-Term Vision: Scaling Your Business

Building a successful mobile notary business is not a static endeavor; it's a dynamic journey of continuous assessment, adaptation, and strategic growth.

Developing a Clear Value Proposition:

- What truly makes your mobile notary service unique and superior? Is it unmatched speed for emergency signings, highly specialized expertise (e.g., complex trust signings, RON capabilities), unparalleled after-hours/weekend availability, a particular geographic focus (e.g., rural areas), or a consistently exceptional customer experience? Clearly articulate this unique selling proposition in all your marketing and communications. This is what differentiates you.

Tracking Your Business Performance (Leads, Revenue, Expenses):

- Implement a simple CRM (Customer Relationship Management) system or even a detailed spreadsheet to track key performance indicators (KPIs). This includes where your leads are coming from (e.g., Google search, NNA locator, specific attorney referral, Facebook ad), your conversion rates, revenue per service type, and all your business expenses. This data is invaluable for understanding which marketing and networking efforts are most effective, allowing you to optimize your time and budget, identify profitable services, and make informed financial decisions.

Adapting and Evolving Continuously:

- The market, technology, and client needs are constantly changing. Continuously assess your marketing strategies: What's working? What's not? Be willing to adapt to market shifts, invest in new skills (e.g., RON commissioning, advanced LSA training), and evolve your service offerings to remain competitive and relevant. This proactive adaptation is crucial for long-term survival and growth.

Considering Team Expansion or Specialization:

- As your business grows and demand for your specialized services increases, you might consider scaling your operations. This could involve bringing on other commissioned notaries to work under your business entity (ensuring proper legal and insurance structures) or hiring administrative support to handle scheduling, marketing, or document preparation. Alternatively, you might choose to deepen your specialization in a very lucrative niche, becoming the undisputed expert in that area.

Conclusion

Marketing and growth are the dynamic, proactive engines that truly drive the growth and sustainability of a mobile notary business. While a robust online presence provides essential visibility, it is through strategic networking with key referral sources, diligent relationship building, and effective direct client acquisition strategies that a notary can ensure a consistent, diverse, and profitable flow of business. By consistently delivering truly exceptional customer service, meticulously tracking performance, and continuously adapting to market demands, you can build an impeccable reputation, diversify your client base, and establish a thriving, sustainable practice in the competitive and ever-evolving mobile notary market. Your ability to connect, communicate, and convert is as vital as your ability to notarize flawlessly, ensuring your blueprint for success becomes a vibrant reality.

Glossary of Key Terms for The Mobile Notary Blueprint

This glossary provides definitions for important terms used throughout "The Mobile Notary Blueprint: Launching and Managing Your On-Demand Business," offering a quick reference to the specialized vocabulary and critical concepts essential for building and managing a successful mobile notary practice.

A

- **Accessibility:** The quality of being easily reached or accessed. For mobile notaries, this refers to providing services to clients regardless of their physical location, mobility challenges, or schedule limitations.
- **Acknowledgments:** A common notarial act where a signer declares they willingly signed a document.
- **Administrative Burden:** The amount of time, effort, and resources required for managing the paperwork, compliance, and record-keeping associated with a business.
- **Ancillary Fees:** Additional charges a mobile notary may levy for services beyond the basic notarial act and travel, such as printing, scanning, or waiting time.
- **Apostille Services:** A specialized service where a notary facilitates the authentication of documents for international use, often involving obtaining an Apostille certificate from the Secretary of State.
- **Automated Buffer Time:** Time automatically added between scheduled appointments by online booking systems to account for travel, preparation, and unexpected delays.
- **Authorized Representative (for I-9):** An individual (often a notary) designated by an employer to complete Section 2 of Form I-9, Employment Eligibility Verification; a non-notarial act.

B

- **Background Check:** A verification of an applicant's criminal history, often required for notary commissioning.
- **Backups (Notary Supplies):** Carrying extra notary stamps, pens, or other essential items to ensure continuity of service in case of malfunction or loss.
- **Batching Appointments:** A scheduling strategy where multiple appointments are grouped together in the same geographical area or along an efficient travel route to minimize unproductive travel time.
- **Behavioral Cues:** Non-verbal or verbal indicators from a signer (e.g., hesitation, evasiveness) that may signal deception or duress.
- **Bond (Notary Bond):** A surety bond required by many states protecting the *public* from financial harm caused by a notary's negligence or misconduct.
- **Branded Email:** A professional email address that uses your business's domain name (e.g., `info@yourbusinessname.com`).
- **Brand Building:** The process of creating and strengthening a positive perception and reputation for your business in the minds of clients.
- **Buffer Time:** Extra time deliberately built into a schedule between appointments to account for unforeseen delays, allowing for punctuality and reduced stress.
- **Business Bank Account:** A dedicated bank account for business finances, crucial for legal separation, tax preparation, and professionalism.
- **Business Cards:** Small, printed cards containing your business name, contact information, and services, used for networking and leaving a professional impression.
- **Business Entity Type:** The legal classification of a business (e.g., Sole Proprietorship, LLC), impacting liability, taxation, and administrative burden.
- **Business Licenses:** Permits or registrations required by state or local governments to legally operate a business.

- **Business Plan:** A roadmap for your business that outlines its model, target market, marketing strategy, and financial projections.

C

- **Calendar Management Systems:** Digital tools (e.g., Google Calendar, Outlook Calendar) used to organize, schedule, and track appointments and tasks efficiently.
- **Cancellation Fees:** Charges levied for appointments canceled without sufficient notice, compensating the notary for lost time and potential revenue.
- **Certificates (Notarial):** The written statement executed by the Notary Public attesting to the facts of a notarial act.
- **Certifying Copies:** A specialized notarial act (permitted in some states for specific documents) where a notary certifies a copy as a true reproduction of an original document.
- **Client Acquisition:** The process of attracting and converting new customers for a business.
- **Client Lifetime Value (CLV):** A prediction of the total revenue a business can expect to generate from a customer throughout their relationship.
- **Client Self-Service:** Empowering clients to perform tasks independently, such as booking appointments online or accessing information on a website.
- **Clipboard/Portable Writing Surface:** A firm, stable surface used for signing documents, especially when a table is unavailable.
- **Cold Outreach:** A proactive client acquisition strategy involving initiating contact with potential clients who have had no prior interaction with your business.
- **Commercial Auto Insurance:** Insurance coverage for vehicles used primarily for business purposes, distinct from personal auto insurance.
- **Commission (Notary):** The official authorization granted by a state government that allows an individual to act as a Notary Public.

- **Commissioning Authority:** The state government office responsible for appointing and regulating Notaries Public (e.g., Secretary of State).
- **Communication (Client):** Clear, proactive, and professional interaction with clients before, during, and after appointments to manage expectations and build trust.
- **Competitive Advantage:** A feature or aspect of your business that makes it superior to competitors, helping you attract and retain clients.
- **Compliance:** Adherence to all relevant laws, regulations, and ethical standards governing notary practice and business operations.
- **Confidentiality:** The ethical and legal obligation to protect signer privacy and sensitive document information.
- **Conflict of Interest:** A situation where a notary has a personal or financial interest in a transaction, compromising impartiality.
- **Content Marketing:** A marketing strategy involving the creation and distribution of valuable, relevant, and consistent content (e.g., blog posts, videos) to attract and retain a clearly defined audience.
- **Convenience:** The primary benefit of mobile notary services, offering ease and flexibility to clients by traveling to their location.
- **Copy Certification:** See **Certifying Copies**.
- **Core Notary Essentials:** The absolute mandatory tools every notary must possess (seal, journal, pens, certificates, handbook).
- **Corporate Resolutions:** Formal decisions made by a company's board of directors or shareholders, often requiring notarization.
- **Courier Services:** A non-notarial service where a notary transports documents or packages for clients.
- **Credibility:** The quality of being trusted and believed in, built through professionalism, compliance, and positive client experiences.

- **Credential Analysis (RON):** Technological process in RON that analyzes security features of a signer's ID against forensic databases.
- **Customer Relationship Management (CRM):** A system or strategy for managing and analyzing customer interactions and data throughout the customer lifecycle.
- **Customer Service:** The support and assistance provided to clients, encompassing all interactions and aiming to ensure satisfaction and build positive relationships.

D

- **Digital Calendars:** See **Calendar Management Systems**.
- **Digital Payment Apps:** Mobile applications (e.g., Venmo, Cash App) that facilitate electronic payments between individuals or businesses.
- **Document Folders/Envelopes:** Supplies used for organizing and protecting signed documents during transport.
- **Document Printing/Scanning Services:** A non-notarial service where a mobile notary offers on-site printing or scanning of documents for clients.
- **Domain Name:** A unique, memorable address for a website on the internet (e.g., `mobilenotarybyderrickspruill.com`).

E

- **Electronic Notarization (eNotary):** A notarial act performed on an electronic document where the notary applies an electronic signature/seal, with the signer in the *physical presence* of the notary.
- **Email Signature:** A block of text automatically appended to outgoing emails, often containing contact information, website links, and branding elements.
- **Employer Identification Number (EIN):** A unique nine-digit tax identification number assigned by the IRS to businesses.
- **Errors & Omissions (E&O) Insurance:** Professional liability insurance that protects the *notary* from financial loss

due to lawsuits arising from unintentional errors or omissions in their duties.

- **ETA (Estimated Time of Arrival):** The projected time a mobile notary expects to arrive at a client's location, communicated proactively to the client.
- **Ethical Driving:** Driving safely and courteously, reflecting positively on a notary's professional image.
- **Ethical Refusal:** The notary's duty and courage to decline a notarization when legal or ethical requirements are not met.

F

- **Facebook Business Page:** A social media platform used for local community engagement, sharing tips, and running targeted local ads.
- **Fees (Notary Act):** The maximum allowable charges a notary can levy for performing notarial acts, strictly regulated by state law.
- **Field Inspections:** A non-notarial service where a notary visits a property to verify occupancy, condition, or other details for clients.
- **Filing Commission:** The process of registering a notary's commission and bond (if applicable) with a county or state office to make it active.
- **Financial Control:** The ability to manage and direct your business's income, expenses, and investments effectively.
- **Fingerprinting Services:** A non-notarial service where a notary provides traditional ink fingerprinting for background checks or licensing.
- **First-Aid Kit:** A basic kit for minor injuries, an essential safety supply for mobile notaries.
- **Flat Fee (Travel):** A single, fixed charge for travel within a specific geographical radius, simplifying pricing.
- **Flexibility:** The ability to adapt to client schedules and locations, a key benefit of mobile notary services.
- **Fraud Prevention:** The active measures employed by notaries to deter, detect, and prevent fraudulent activities.

G

- **General Liability Insurance:** Business insurance protecting against claims of bodily injury or property damage to a third party during business operations.
- **Geographical Batching:** A scheduling strategy to group multiple appointments in the same area to optimize travel time and costs.
- **Google My Business (GMB) Profile:** A free tool from Google that allows businesses to manage their online presence across Google Search and Maps, crucial for local SEO.
- **GPS/Navigation:** Tools (e.g., Google Maps, Waze) used for optimal route planning and accurate navigation to client locations.

H

- **High-Quality Pens:** Pens using archival-quality, permanent, non-smearing ink, essential for legible and long-lasting notary marks.
- **High-Value Appointments:** Notarizations (e.g., loan signings, apostille services) that command higher fees due to complexity or specialization.
- **Home-Based Business Permits:** Local permits or zoning approvals required for operating a business primarily from a residential property.
- **Hotspot (Mobile):** A device or smartphone feature providing portable internet access, crucial for on-the-go operations.

I

- **ID Card Reader:** An optional tool for advanced identity verification, electronically reading data from identification documents.
- **Identity Verification Aids:** Specialized tools (e.g., magnifying glass, UV light, ID card reader) that enhance a notary's ability to scrutinize identification documents.

- **Impartiality:** The notary's unbiased, neutral stance in all notarial acts, crucial for credibility.
- **Indemnification (Bond):** The legal right of a surety company to seek reimbursement from the notary after paying a bond claim.
- **Initial Investment:** The upfront costs associated with setting up a new business, including equipment, supplies, and initial registrations.
- **Invoicing App/Software:** Tools for creating and sending professional, itemized invoices to clients.
- **I-9 Verification:** A non-notarial service where a notary acts as an Authorized Representative for an employer to verify an employee's identity and employment authorization.

J

- **Journal (Notary Journal):** A chronological, permanent record of all notarial acts performed by a notary, serving as an audit trail and defense.
- **Jurat:** A notarial act where a signer swears/affirms to a document's truthfulness and signs *in the notary's presence.*

K

- **Knowledge-Based Authentication (KBA):** Technological identity verification in RON where a signer answers personal questions from data sources.

L

- **Laptop/Tablet:** Portable computing devices essential for managing business operations, accessing electronic documents, and performing digital notarizations.
- **Legal Entity Type:** The chosen legal structure for a business (e.g., Sole Proprietorship, LLC), impacting liability and taxes.
- **Legal Presumption of Authenticity:** The legal principle that a properly notarized document is presumed to be genuine.

- **Liability:** Legal responsibility for one's actions or omissions, leading to potential harm or loss.
- **Limited Liability Company (LLC):** A business structure providing personal liability protection to its owners.
- **Loan Signing Agent (LSA):** A specialized notary guiding borrowers through real estate loan documents.
- **Local SEO:** Search Engine Optimization strategies focused on improving a business's visibility in local search results.
- **Loose Notarial Certificates:** Blank, state-compliant notary certificates attached to documents lacking proper pre-printed certificates.

M

- **Magnifying Glass:** Tool for scrutinizing tiny details and security features on IDs.
- **Marketing:** The process of promoting and selling products or services, including market research and advertising.
- **Medical Documents:** Legal papers related to healthcare decisions (e.g., Advance Healthcare Directives), often requiring notarization.
- **Meticulous Record Keeping:** Diligent practice of maintaining accurate, complete, and chronological notary journal records.
- **Micro-printing:** Tiny text security feature on IDs, visible under magnification.
- **Ministerial Act:** A duty performed by a public official (like a notary) that does not involve exercising discretion or interpreting legal principles.
- **Mobile Card Reader:** A device allowing notaries to accept credit/debit card payments on the spot.
- **Mobile Hotspot:** See **Hotspot (Mobile)**.
- **Mobile Notary:** A Notary Public who travels to a client's preferred location.
- **Mobile Office Setup:** The collection of essential tools and supplies that enable a notary to perform duties efficiently and professionally on the go.

- **Multi-Stop Routing:** A navigation feature that optimizes a route for multiple appointments, minimizing travel time.

N

- **Networking:** The proactive process of building and maintaining professional relationships for mutual benefit, often leading to referrals.
- **Notarial Act:** An official, legally authorized act performed by a notary (e.g., Acknowledgment, Jurat).
- **Notarial Certificate:** The written statement by the notary attesting to the facts of a notarial act.
- **Notary Bond:** See **Bond (Notary Bond)**.
- **Notary Journal:** See **Journal (Notary Journal)**.
- **Notary Public:** Individual commissioned by a state to serve as an impartial witness and administrator of oaths.

O

- **Oath:** A solemn promise to tell the truth, administered by the notary.
- **On-Demand Service:** Services available to clients when and where they need them, a hallmark of mobile notary work.
- **Online Booking Systems:** Software allowing clients to view availability and book appointments directly, automating scheduling.
- **Online Presence:** A business's digital footprint across the internet (website, social media, directories).
- **Operational Efficiency:** The ability to perform duties and manage processes effectively and without waste, maximizing productivity.
- **Operational Excellence:** A proactive commitment to the highest standards of practice, characterized by precision, diligence, and continuous improvement in notary duties.
- **Opportunity Cost:** The value of the next best alternative that was not taken when a decision was made (e.g., lost billable time during travel).

- **Organizational Supplies:** General office supplies (e.g., paper clips, stapler, folders) for maintaining order in a mobile office.
- **Originals Only (ID):** The requirement to physically examine original identification documents, not copies, for verification.

P

- **Paper Clips:** Organizational supplies for documents.
- **Parental consent:** A legal document, often notarized, granting explicit permission for a minor child to travel.
- **Payment Integration:** Connecting online booking systems or websites with payment processing services.
- **Payment Methods:** Various ways clients can pay for services (e.g., cash, check, credit card, digital apps).
- **Payment Processing Tools:** Systems (e.g., mobile card readers, invoicing apps) that facilitate accepting and tracking client payments.
- **Pens (High-Quality):** Essential notary supplies using approved, permanent ink.
- **Per Signature Fee:** The fee charged for each individual notarial act, typically capped by state law.
- **Personal Appearance:** Requirement for signer to be physically (or virtually for RON) present before the notary.
- **Personal Liability Protection:** Legal safeguards (e.g., LLC structure) that separate an owner's personal assets from business debts and lawsuits.
- **Personal Safety Measures:** Protocols and habits implemented by notaries to ensure their security during appointments.
- **Portable Printer/Scanner:** A compact, mobile device for printing and scanning documents on the go.
- **Post-Appointment Follow-Up:** Communication with clients after a service to ensure satisfaction and encourage reviews.
- **Pricing Strategy:** The method used to determine and structure fees for services, balancing costs, value, and market competitiveness.
- **Professional Attire:** Appropriate clothing and appearance for a notary, conveying professionalism and trustworthiness.

- **Professional Briefcase/Notary Bag:** A sturdy, organized bag for safely carrying notary supplies and documents.
- **Professional Email Address:** An email address using your business's domain name, enhancing credibility.
- **Professionalism:** The conduct, qualities, and ethical standards that characterize a professional notary.
- **Profitability:** The ability of a business to generate revenue in excess of its expenses, leading to financial gain.
- **Promissory Note:** A legal document outlining a borrower's promise to repay a loan, often found in loan packages.
- **Prohibited Acts:** Actions a notary is legally forbidden from performing.
- **Public Trust:** The confidence placed by the public in the integrity and impartiality of a notary.
- **Punctuality:** The quality of being on time for appointments, a key aspect of professionalism and client satisfaction.

R

- **Real Estate Agents:** Professionals who facilitate property transactions and are often referral sources for notaries.
- **Real Estate Closings:** The final stage of a property transaction where ownership is transferred and financial agreements are finalized.
- **Receipt Book:** A physical book for providing handwritten receipts for payments.
- **Record Keeping:** The diligent practice of maintaining accurate, complete, and chronological records of all notarial acts.
- **Red Flags:** Warning signs indicating potential fraud, duress, or other issues.
- **Referral Programs:** Formal systems to incentivize clients or professionals to send new business.
- **Referral Source:** A professional or client who sends new business to a notary.
- **Refusal to Notarize:** Notary's right and duty to decline an act when legal/ethical requirements are not met.

- **Remote Online Notarization (RON):** Notarization performed virtually via secure audio-visual technology.
- **Reputation:** The public perception of a notary's reliability, trustworthiness, and professionalism.
- **Residential Lease Agreement:** A contract outlining terms for renting a residential property.
- **Responsiveness:** The speed and efficiency with which a notary responds to client inquiries and needs.
- **Reviews (Online):** Client feedback posted on platforms like Google My Business or Yelp, crucial for reputation and marketing.
- **Route planning:** The process of determining the most efficient and safe travel routes for mobile notary appointments.
- **"Rush Job" (Psychological Tactic):** A fraudster tactic where urgency is created to pressure the notary.

S

- **Safety:** The paramount concern for a notary's personal security and well-being during appointments.
- **Satisfactory Evidence (of Identity):** Acceptable forms of identification that assure the notary of a signer's identity.
- **Scheduling:** The process of managing and organizing appointments, crucial for mobile notaries.
- **Seal (Notary Seal):** The official stamp or embosser used by a notary to authenticate their acts.
- **Secure Document Handling:** Practices to protect sensitive documents from unauthorized access or damage.
- **Security Features (ID):** Embedded elements in identification documents (e.g., holograms, UV features) designed to prevent counterfeiting.
- **Self-Motivation:** The drive and initiative to manage one's own business effectively.
- **Service Area:** The defined geographical region where a mobile notary offers their services.

- **Service-Specific Booking:** Allowing clients to book different types of notary services with varying time allocations and pricing.
- **Signer Awareness:** The notary's assessment that a signer understands the document and notarial act.
- **Signer Willingness:** The notary's assessment that a signer is acting voluntarily, without duress.
- **Signing Agent Websites/Platforms:** Online platforms used by title companies and signing services to assign loan closings to LSAs.
- **Sole Proprietorship:** A business structure where the owner is personally liable for all business debts.
- **Specialized Expertise:** In-depth knowledge and skills in specific notary niches (e.g., loan signings, apostille services).
- **Specialized Service Fees:** Higher fees charged for complex or niche notary services.
- **Stapler/Staple Remover:** Organizational supplies for documents.
- **State Notary Handbook:** Official reference guide for notary laws and procedures in a specific state.
- **State-Specific Notary Laws:** The unique laws governing notaries in each U.S. state.
- **Sticky Notes/Flags:** Organizational supplies for marking document pages.
- **Strategic Growth:** Planned expansion and development of a business to achieve long-term success.
- **Structuring Fees:** The process of determining and organizing charges for notary services.
- **Surety (Bond):** The bonding company that issues a notary bond.
- **Sympathy (Psychological Tactic):** A fraudster tactic appealing to a notary's emotions to bypass rules.

T

- **Tamper-Evident:** A characteristic that makes any unauthorized alteration to a document or record detectable.

- **Target Referral Sources:** Professionals or businesses who frequently need notary services and are ideal for networking.
- **Tax Implications:** How business structure and income affect tax obligations.
- **Testimonials:** Positive statements from satisfied clients, used as social proof in marketing.
- **Tiered Fee (Travel):** A travel fee structure where charges increase based on mileage ranges from the notary's base location.
- **Time-Based (Travel Fee):** A travel fee structure where charges are based on the actual time spent traveling.
- **Time-Saving:** A key benefit of mobile notary services for clients, as it eliminates their need to travel and wait.
- **Title Company:** In real estate transactions, a company that conducts title searches and issues title insurance.
- **Tracking (Business Performance):** Monitoring key performance indicators (KPIs) like leads, revenue, and expenses.
- **Training (Notary):** Education required or recommended for notary applicants or commissioned notaries.
- **Transparency (Fees):** Clearly communicating all charges to the client upfront to avoid misunderstandings.
- **Travel documents:** Legal documents related to personal and family affairs, often involving travel, such as parental consent forms for minors.
- **Travel fees:** Additional charges levied by mobile notaries to compensate for their time, mileage, and expenses incurred traveling to a client's location.
- **Trust:** The confidence and reliance placed by the public in the integrity, impartiality, and competence of a notary public.
- **Trustee (Trusts):** The individual or entity responsible for managing assets within a trust for beneficiaries.

U

- **Unauthorized Practice of Law (UPL):** Performance of legal services by non-attorneys, strictly prohibited for notaries.

- **Undue influence:** Improper use of power to deprive a person of free will. Notaries must guard against this.
- **Unexpired IDs:** Identification documents that are still valid and have not passed their expiration date, required for notarization.
- **Unsuitable Environment:** A location for notarization that is too dark, noisy, public, or otherwise compromises the notary's ability to perform duties or ensure safety.
- **U.S. Citizenship and Immigration Services (USCIS):** Federal agency overseeing immigration and Form I-9.
- **UV Light (Ultraviolet Light):** A tool used to check ultraviolet security features on identification documents and currency.

V

- **Value Proposition:** A clear statement that articulates the unique benefits, value, or solutions a business offers to its clients.
- **Vehicle Maintenance:** Regular upkeep of a notary's vehicle, crucial for reliability and professionalism.
- **Vehicle title transfers:** Legal documents used to legally transfer ownership of a motor vehicle.
- **Venue (Notary Certificate):** The geographical location (state and county) where a notarial act physically takes place.
- **Vigilance:** The state of being watchful, alert, and attentive to potential dangers or red flags.
- **Vital records:** Official government documents (e.g., birth certificates) notaries are generally prohibited from copy-certifying.

W

- **Waiting Fees:** Charges for time spent waiting for a client beyond a predetermined grace period.
- **Website (Professional):** An online presence serving as a business's digital storefront and information hub.

- **Willingness and Awareness:** Two critical elements a notary public must assess in every signer before performing a notarial act.
- **Witness (Document Witness):** An individual who observes a signer affix their signature to a document, often required by legal documents in addition to the notary.
- **Witness Provided Fee:** A separate fee a mobile notary may charge for arranging and providing disinterested witnesses.
- **Work-Life Balance:** The ability to manage professional and personal responsibilities effectively, often enhanced by flexible mobile notary work.

Z

- **Zoning Laws:** Local regulations that govern land use and may impact where a home-based business can operate.

About the Author: Derrick Spruill

Derrick Spruill is not just an author; he is a **highly respected Notary Public**, a **certified Loan Signing Agent (LSA)**, and the visionary **founder of Mobile Notary by Derrick Spruill**. Based in Herndon, Virginia, Derrick has meticulously built a career grounded in unwavering integrity, meticulous professionalism, and a profound commitment to public service. His journey into the notary profession began with a clear vision: to provide convenient, reliable, and expert notarization services that genuinely meet the demands of modern life.

Derrick's hands-on experience as a mobile notary has provided him with unparalleled, real-world insights into the operational intricacies of a notary practice. He has personally executed countless notarial acts, from high-stakes real estate closings to critical estate planning documents, giving him a deep understanding of the precision required for certificates, journals, ink, and copy certification. This practical expertise forms the authentic foundation of his educational mission.

With an **MBA in Human Resources and a bachelor's degree in accounting from Walden University**, Derrick seamlessly combines his robust educational background with **over 25 years of experience working for Fortune 100 companies**. This unique blend of academic rigor and extensive corporate experience provides him with invaluable insights into business operations, process optimization, and the critical role of meticulous compliance—all principles central to achieving operational excellence in the notary field. He passionately shares this knowledge with his readers and clients.

Beyond his direct client services and business acumen, Derrick is deeply committed to community service and helping individuals in need. This dedication led him to establish Mobile Notary by Derrick Spruill. He is a passionate educator and mentor, sharing his expertise to help others navigate the complexities of the notary profession. He is the creator of the acclaimed **"Notary Knowledge by Derrick Spruill" podcast**, hosted by Eddie and Marylyn where they share practical advice, critical ethical insights, and timely industry updates with a growing audience of aspiring and active notaries. His dedication to empowering others is further solidified through his comprehensive **"Notary Knowledge: The Complete Guide Series,"** a collection designed to elevate every notary's practice.

Derrick firmly believes that a notary's role transcends merely applying a stamp; it is a **vital public trust** that demands continuous education, unwavering ethical vigilance, and an unyielding dedication to protecting the integrity of every document. His commitment to serving others is deeply rooted in the values instilled by his parents and the constant inspiration from his wife, who remains his greatest support. Looking ahead, Derrick is also building on the fantastic world of Little Notary Derrick, aiming to bring notary knowledge to an even broader and younger audience, fostering an early understanding of integrity and civic duty.

In his free time, Derrick enjoys expanding his knowledge by reading about business, following the thrilling world of NASCAR, and passionately cheering on his favorite NFL team, the Cincinnati Bengals. He and his wife reside in Herndon, Virginia.

Derrick Spruill's Core Values

Derrick's professional and personal life are guided by these foundational principles:

- **Service First:** He believes the notary's highest calling is to serve the public with integrity, impartiality, and a genuine desire to assist.
- **Knowledge is Power:** A notary's strongest defense against risk and fraud is a deep, continuously updated understanding of state law, best practices, and emerging industry trends.
- **Professionalism is Non-Negotiable:** Every interaction, every document, and every client presents an opportunity to reinforce trust, build a stellar reputation, and exemplify the highest standards of the profession.

- **Embrace the Future:** Notaries must adapt to and master new technologies, such as Remote Online Notarization (RON) and Electronic Notarization (eNotary), to remain relevant, indispensable, and efficient in an increasingly digital world.
- **Integrity Above All:** Upholding ethical standards and maintaining unwavering honesty are paramount to the public trust placed in the notary office.

Derrick Spruill's Goals

Derrick is driven by a clear vision for the notary profession:

- **Empower Notaries:** To equip every notary, from novice to veteran, with the comprehensive knowledge and practical skills needed to perform their duties flawlessly and confidently.
- **Elevate the Profession:** To raise the standards of notary practice across the industry, fostering a community of highly competent, ethical, and respected professionals.
- **Combat Fraud:** To serve as a leading voice and resource in the fight against document fraud and identity theft, protecting individuals and the integrity of critical transactions.
- **Promote Accessibility:** To ensure that essential notary services are accessible and convenient for all individuals, regardless of their location or physical limitations, through mobile and digital solutions.
- **Inspire Future Notaries:** To ignite a passion for public service and legal integrity in the next generation, including through engaging content like "Little Notary Derrick."

Books by Derrick Spruill

Derrick Spruill is the author of the comprehensive "Notary Knowledge: Reference Guide & Notary Bible" and the following complementary books, designed to provide focused, in-depth exploration of key areas within the notary profession:

- **Notary Knowledge: Reference Guide & Notary Bible**

- **The Notary Public Foundation: Your Essential Guide to Core Duties, Ethics, and Commissioning**
- **Notary Operational Excellence: Mastering Certificates, Journals, Ink, and Copy Certification**
- **Notary Fraud Shield: Real-World Tactics, Red Flags, and Refusal Strategies**
- **The Mobile Notary Blueprint: Launching and Managing Your On-Demand Business**
- **Notary Niche Navigator: Your Guide to Loan Signings, Apostilles, I-9s, and More**
- **Notary Law & Liability: Understanding State Regulations, Insurance, and Avoiding UPL**
- **The Future Notary: Mastering RON, eNotary, and Complex Scenarios**
- **Quick & Easy Solutions: How to Increase Mobile Notary Business for More Success & Profit**
- **Learning with Derrick Activity Books** (Series)
- **Little Notary Derrick Children's Books** (Series)

End Notes

As we conclude **"The Mobile Notary Blueprint: Launching and Managing Your On-Demand Business,"** I want to express my sincere hope that this guide has empowered you with the practical knowledge and unwavering confidence needed to build your thriving mobile notary enterprise. My journey with Mobile Notary by Derrick Spruill has shown me the immense potential of this on-demand service, and I am truly excited for you to embark on your own path to success.

Remember, launching and managing a mobile notary business is a dynamic endeavor. It requires meticulous planning in your legal and financial foundations, thoughtful investment in your mobile office, strategic pricing, and, crucially, a relentless commitment to operational excellence and exceptional client service. Your ability to connect, communicate, and deliver seamlessly is what will set you apart.

Keep these final thoughts at the forefront of your practice:

- **Build on Solid Ground:** Ensure your business structure, licenses, and insurance are meticulously in place from day one.
- **Equip for Excellence:** Your tools are extensions of your professionalism. Invest wisely and keep them organized.
- **Price Your Value:** Understand your worth, calculate your costs, and communicate your fees transparently.
- **Master the Flow:** Efficient scheduling and seamless logistics are the heartbeat of your mobile business.
- **Serve and Grow:** Exceptional customer service is your ultimate marketing tool, fostering loyalty and referrals.

The mobile notary revolution is here to stay, and you are now equipped to be a leader within it. Embrace continuous learning, stay vigilant against challenges, and never forget the profound public trust placed in your hands.

Thank you for allowing me to share this blueprint with you. I wish you unparalleled success, unwavering professionalism, and deep fulfillment in every notarization you perform.

— Derrick Spruill

www.ingramcontent.com/pod-product-compliance
Lightning Source LLC
Chambersburg PA
CBHW071350230926
51846CB00002B/495
* 9 7 8 1 9 6 5 8 9 6 1 9 8 *